Walking Through the Valleys of Life

Jerry W. Beaver

WALKING THROUGH THE VALLEYS OF LIFE

Walking Through the Valleys of Life is a book that is practical, applicable, and Biblically sound. ~Dr. David C. Gibbs, Jr.

Printing/Year 2009
All Scriptures are quoted from the KJV Bible
ISBN-13: 978-0-615-27688-5
ISBN-10: 0-615-27688-1
Copyright 2009

Acknowledgments

There is an endless list of people that have helped me in the completion of this book. First, I would like to thank my Lord and Saviour, Who saved me from a miserable life and gave me a new life in Him. Also, I would like to thank Him for all my valleys that He has allowed, because they have produced a deeper faith in my walk with Christ. I would like to thank my Pastor, Dewey Weaver, for leading me to Christ and being the one that God used in my life to show me true faithfulness to the Lord. Last, but by no means the least, I want to thank my wife, who has stood by me in the valleys and loved me, also for the hours of work and encouragement that she has given throughout the process of not only this book but also in the ministry.

A Special Thanks to Jeanette Hanscome for Editing

Contents

Introduction

*A*fter a church service one Sunday, a man came forward to pray at the altar call. A deacon approached the man as he was praying, and he was weeping bitterly, so the deacon knelt down to pray with him. Putting his hand on the man's back, the deacon overheard a prayer like this: "Lord, I hate flour; it is bland and chokes me. Lord, I hate plain butter, and I hate baking soda and salt by itself. But Lord, I love fresh biscuits. And Lord, just like I hate all those individual biscuit ingredients by themselves, I hate the particular problems that are in my life right now. Just like making biscuits, Lord, I believe my trials and burdens will turn out for the good when You put them all together."

What a great illustration of life. Many of the individual problems in our lives are very hard and cumbersome, and we really don't like them at first. However, when the situations are all put together, God brings them together for something beautiful in our lives in the end. Isaiah 61:3 says, "to give unto them beauty for ashes, the oil of joy for mourning, the garment of praise for the spirit of heaviness; that they might be called trees of righteousness, the planting of the LORD…"

If we live in this world, we know that life can be difficult. Often life is one sorrowful valley after another. These valleys can be defined as trials, tests, situations, or circumstances, which seem to go on forever. In these valleys, we find that there are great hurts, but we see also a cavern of blessings in the same valleys, from the result of God's handiwork in our lives. Looking back in hindsight, if we could have seen this outcome of blessings, and if we could have kept our minds focused on the blessings during all the valleys, then our lives and walk through these trials would have been totally different.

Now that I have stated the obvious, I am going to go ahead and tell you what the secret is for making this happen in your life. Whether you're grieving the loss of a loved one, you're terminally ill, suffering from depression, jobless, full of anger, suffering under abuse, or suffering in some other way, the answer is found in God and His Son the Lord Jesus Christ. We must see and believe that God has made us and gave us life, and that He is likewise able to get us through this life. He has desired to have a relationship with us, lead us, protect us, and love us through this world in which we live. He has not left us to survive on our own. If you're reading this and you're wondering if you can make it, let me assure you by the power of God that you can!

CHAPTER 1

THE VALLEY OF PURPOSE

Here I was a Christian, in the middle of my life, hurting and fearful. At the same time, I felt ashamed because I doubted whether or not the Lord was still with me in the darkest time of my life. I looked for Him, but I could not see Him. I called for Him, but His voice I could not hear. But the gloriousness of this time came when God led me through the valley. I found that He had been speaking and leading me all along, and as a result, my faith in Him was stronger than before.

Sincerely,
A Struggling, but Victorious Christian

The Shepherd and Sheep Relationship

Valleys have the power to grow and mature us. However, in the stress of the struggle, we often make some of the worst mistakes of our lives. We look back at our choices and ask, "What in the world was I thinking?" It then becomes apparent that we were not thinking clearly during those tumultuous times.

The questions that we need to ponder are:

Is this the way God intended for us to live our lives?

Is this the way we want to continue to live in the future?

Meaning, *Are people's lives just tossed around with every valley that comes?* I believe that I can answer that question for you. NO! The reason that I answer so firmly is because of the promises that we find so clearly declared in the Scriptures concerning those who are His children and sheep. We don't have to be sinking in the valleys and making bad decisions, but we can be looking up to the Lord. Seeing the greatness of our Shepherd and Saviour helps us to live victoriously, even when troubles arise. This hopeful life in the Lord, our Shepherd, can become engrained in our relationship with the Him. You may say, "I am saved, and I love the Lord, but what you just said does not describe my life." Well, bear with me, and I think by the end of this book your perspective will have changed.

The Twenty-third Psalm so clearly and dearly illustrates a victorious life in the Lord.

The LORD is my shepherd; I shall not want. He maketh me to lie down in green pastures: he leadeth me beside the still waters. He restoreth my soul: he leadeth me in the paths of righteousness for his name's sake. Yea, though I walk through the valley of the shadow of death, I will fear no evil: for thou art with me; thy rod and thy staff they comfort me. Thou preparest a table before me in the presence of mine enemies: thou anointest my head with oil; my cup runneth over. Surely goodness and mercy shall follow me all the days of my life: and I will dwell in the house of the LORD for ever.

Psalms 23:1-6

This particular text is one of the best known passages of Scripture. Just about every funeral that I have ever done or have ever been to has used this Psalm. In my opinion, Psalm 23 is the most widely recognized Bible passage. Though this portion of Scripture is used in funerals, unfortunately, this Scripture has very little to do with death, but it does have much to do with our lives as followers of the Lord Jesus Christ, the Great Shepherd.

As we look at Psalm 23:1, it says, "The Lord is my shepherd; I shall not want." The first part of the text gives an illustration of a shepherd and a sheep. In this shepherd and sheep relationship, we know that the shepherd is the protector and the leader of the sheep. He is their caretaker, and these sheep need him desperately. The shepherd could easily exist without the sheep; however, it would be hard, if not impossible, for the sheep to exist without the shepherd.

The shepherd loves and lives for the sheep. He puts his life on the line for them, as did David fighting the bears and lions in the wilderness. Without the shepherd, the sheep can be found hanging off a cliff and eating little scraps of grass. Sheep without a shepherd are mistakenly even called goats at times. The wild sheep, or goats with no shepherd, are a perfect representation of a child of God who has walked away from the Lord, or an unsaved person who has no Saviour. These spiritual wild sheep look and act more like wild goats than sheep of the Great Shepherd.

> One's identity, as a sheep of the Great Shepherd, is vitally important for walking through the valleys.

In contrast, when you see the tame sheep with their shepherd, you see them out in a bountiful field eating knee-high grass, and the sheep are fat and sassy. Unlike the skinny, unprotected sheep, those who stick close to their shepherd enjoy peace and security in the midst of danger and darkness. As you examine your relationship with the Lord, do these statements describe your life? By the end of reading this book, I hope and believe that it will.

In essence, and illustrated in our lives, God is saying in Psalm 23:1, "I am their Shepherd, and MY SHEEP shall not want at all if they are in a proper relationship with Me." God knows how to provide for our needs in all areas of our lives because He is our Shepherd and we are His sheep.

One's identity, as a sheep of the Great Shepherd, is vitally important for walking through the valleys. If you do not know the Lord as your Saviour, then you cannot claim the promises given by the Shepherd found in Psalm 23. They are exclusive to followers of Christ. If you are a follower of the Shepherd, this relationship and truth affords you great opportunities and a proper perspective of life. Thus, as a result of who I am in Christ, my relationship dictates my actions, my claiming the great promises, and how they apply to me. Jesus speaks to this end in John 15:5, "...for without me ye can do nothing." Paul also attests to these promises in Philippians 4:13, "I can do all things through Christ which strengtheneth me."

Many people have assumed that maybe David wrote this Psalm while he was a shepherd. I believe that it was written either during his flight from Saul, or when Absalom, his son, had over thrown his kingdom and was trying to kill him.

I personally believe, as this Psalm was being written, under the inspiration of the Lord, David remembered back to the time when he loved, provided, and cared for his sheep, at times, risking his life to protect them. Then, from this reflection and comparing his present turmoil with God's love for him as his Shepherd, there was born this great passage of Scripture.

As illustrated in the life of this shepherd and sheep relationship, some of the basic needs of natural sheep are similar to the needs we have as Christians. The sheep need guidance, food, and protection. When they get sick or injured, the sheep need healing. "He maketh me to lie down in green pastures: he leadeth me beside the still waters (Psalms 23:2), "...thou anointest my head with oil; my cup runneth over" (v.5). As spiritual sheep, we need guidance, the Bread of Life, the protection by the sovereignty of God, and healing of our souls through salvation.

God, being our Shepherd, knows how to protect and make provision for His children. God promises in Matthew 6:28, "And why take ye thought for raiment? Consider the lilies of the field, how they grow; they toil not, neither do they spin:" and in Matthew 6:32-34,

(For after all these things do the Gentiles seek:) for your heavenly Father knoweth that ye have need of all these things. But seek ye first the kingdom of God, and his righteousness; and all these things shall be added unto you. Take therefore no thought for the morrow: for the morrow shall take thought for the things of itself. Sufficient unto the day is the evil thereof.

If only we could live these verses on a daily basis? How different life would be! But let me remind us that God intends that we do live out these verses. Unfortunately, in spite of the Great Shepherd and His blessings to us as sheep, we can and do move out of the place of the Shepherd's care in many of the trials and valleys that we face, and then, consequently, there come problems and danger for us. I have seen too many of God's people that I love and admire give up on God during difficult times. They give up on the church, give up on serving God, quit their marriages and file for divorce, give up on life after they lose a loved one, or become a hermit after the loss of a career. These people forget that God is with them, ready to protect, lead, and provide for them because He is their Shepherd. Some good questions for one to ponder are: How is my valley affecting me? Am I aware that the Lord is with me? What about my valleys in the past? How have I weathered them? Have I looked to the Lord, knowing He would provide, or have I been doubtful and lacking faith?

David again illustrates God's knowledge of our needs in verse number two, "He maketh me to lie down in green pastures: He leadeth me beside the still waters." In the illustration, there are some specific details given of God's great provisions. Sheep, lying down in these green pastures, portray the picture of the assurance given to them of the Shepherd's fold, which is the assurance of great peace, provisions, and protection by the Shepherd. The second part of the provisions of verse two states, "He leadeth me beside the still waters."

The reason these two particular provisions are important is that when we study sheep, it reveals that these animals can be very timid creatures. If you were to yell at them loudly, the sheep would flinch in terror and either freeze or run for safety. Likewise, sheep are very finicky when it comes to their food, in comparison to goats, which will eat just about anything. (The goats here picture the unsaved of the world who don't have their faith in the Lord.)

Throughout the time period of the writing of Psalm Twenty-three, the sheep and goats were herded together. In the New Testament, Jesus speaks of the sheep and the goats, and how that they will be separated on the Day of Judgment. According to the book, *Manners & Customs of Bible Times*, "There are a number of differences between the two animals. Goats are generally dark and sheep are white:"[1] One can visibly see the difference between the sheep and the goats. There must be a distinction between us as God's sheep and the goats of the world, especially in the valleys of life. From a distance, you could easily identify the white wool of the sheep. How is this difference reflected in our lives? When people watch our responses to crisis, what do they see? Do our actions and reactions identify us as sheep of the Great Shepherd?

The provisions from the Shepherd being listed in verse two is a positive for the sheep but a negative for the Shepherd. As sheep are finicky, they will not drink from water that is rushing because rushing water frightens them, and so they will refuse to drink. The finicky sheep, likewise, are not physically able to climb steep rocks to get food like the goats. So, they need food that is laid out for them.

> Christians can be very negative, wanting things their way or no way.

This need of convenience for the sheep brings about a negative for the shepherd because he has to find nice quality grass for the sheep as well as water that is smooth flowing so that the sheep will drink from it, while at the same time, he must still be concerned about keeping the sheep safe. The Shepherd, here in verse two, promises to provide great food and water for the sheep if the sheep will follow Him as He leads them to the place of the provisions.

The positive for us, as the spiritual sheep of the Lord, is that God will lead us to the provisions we need, and at times, He will even give us the desires of our hearts. He will work with us and train us to trust in Him.

We can sit in big bountiful fields and eat grass at the protection of the Shepherd, as well, we can be led to the Living Water, in which we will never thirst again (John 4:13). The alternative is to stop trusting and following the Lord and be like the goats of the world that are eating the scraps that the Devil dishes out.

Unfortunately, like physical sheep that are hard to please,

Christians are the same way. Christians can be very negative, wanting things their way or no way. For example, God can bless a Christian's life for many, many years with health, family, and finances. However, when the least little problem arises, they forget all the years of blessings. Thus, many times, they stop trusting and following because things are not perfect. Christians expect the water of their lives to be just right and grass in their fields made to order. People are so accustomed to the fast food restaurants and other services delivering their food the way they ordered it, or they get upset. Similarly, when life is just not what we think it should be, we get upset with God and life.

Our lives are not made to order according to our tastes; but instead, they are planned out and provided for, according to God's will for us. God knows our needs, our desires, and fears. Sometimes, He works with us and gives us what we want, but He always gives us what we need. Often, the trouble comes when what we think we need differs from what God knows we need. We think we need more than we actually do. If God does not give us those needs that we want fulfilled, He will change our perspective about our real needs and His provisions, if we allow Him.

The grass in the valley is just as nutritious as the grass in the fields, and many times, even more so because of the water that settles in the bottom of the valley. Our Shepherd will provide for us, and He will give us all things, if they coincide with His will and what is best for us.

For example, at times, wolves will hide in tall grass or even at the calm streams. A person who is a hunter knows that the secret to hunting wild game is to find their food and/or water source, and then he will find the wild game. Satan, our enemy at large, observes us on a day-to-day basis, looking to destroy us and get us out of the will of God. So, there are times in our lives when God says, "You cannot eat over there, no matter how good the grass looks," because He knows it is dangerous for the sheep.

A perfect example of this is marrying an unsaved or unspiritual person. You may think you can win them to the Lord, but God knows better. God knows the dangers ahead, of being unequally yoked, that you cannot see because you are blinded by love.

God always determines whether things are either right or wrong for us, based on our sanctification (not whether it feels satisfying at the time) and His will for our lives. When something fits these qualifications, our Shepherd is more than happy to give us all things, as He states in Psalms 84:11, "For the LORD God is a sun and shield: the LORD will give grace and glory: no good thing will he withhold from them that walk uprightly." This truth reminds me of the story of the feeding of the four thousand, in Mark 8:3. When Jesus saw the people who had been with Him three days, and that they had nothing to eat, He said, "And if I send them away fasting to their own houses, they will faint by the way: for divers of them came from far." God actually decided and decreed based on the needs of the people, and He catered His will for His disciples to provide for the people.

God will do this, at times, for His people; but we have no right to demand Him to direct our lives according to our perceived needs. Too many times, we try to guide our lives by our feelings or fancies. The Shepherd needs to be in control and be followed in order for us, as sheep, to get the provisions that we truly need. How have you perceived the Lord's provisions for your life? Have you been guilty of complaining about the Shepherd's provisions?

Look at the very next verse, number three, "He restoreth my soul: He leadeth me in the paths of righteousness for His name's sake." Our Shepherd and Saviour knows His will, our needs, and our wants. He says, "He leadeth me in the paths of righteousness for His name's sake."

Here, righteousness has a two-fold definition. One, it is holiness towards God, and two, right living. The path to the provisions of the Shepherd is paved with the stones that make us right with the Lord. Our Shepherd knows how to work in our lives and how to lead us in the way which He would have us to go for His name's sake. Righteousness is always a primary purpose in our lives, and His will is the only way for the sheep to find true purpose and meaning in life.

> Righteousness is always a primary purpose in our lives, and His will is the only way for the sheep to find true purpose and meaning in life.

This path, for many of us, may even be in a dark valley for a prolonged period.

The Valley

The central verse of Psalm 23, in my opinion, is verse 4. This states, "Yea..." (which means "yes"), "though I walk..." (which means I'm going to walk), "through the valley of the shadow of death..." But look at the end result. "I will fear no evil: for Thou art with me; Thy rod and Thy staff they comfort me."

Interestingly enough, God says, "You're going to walk through the valley." The word valley, as we defined earlier, is a trial, test, situation, or circumstance that is prolonged in our lives.

Note that, up until this part of the chapter, this Psalm has been remarkably positive. God seemly has been leading His sheep in great blessings and provisions. However, here, we see a little change of scenario; but, do not miss that this is still a part of the great blessings from our Shepherd.

To forget this truth when tragedy hits, often causes us to question God. We will say, "I thought You loved me God, and You promised to take care of me?" God's love for us is never in question. No matter what our circumstances say or how we feel, God never stops loving His children, but the details sometimes get in the way of our understanding.

There are a couple of thoughts on why we must experience valleys during our lives. The first thought is that, *I may have been the one who walked away from the Shepherd in the bountiful fields of His provisions.* Elmer Towns writes in his book, *Praying the Twenty-Third Psalm*, "How did you end up in a dark valley full of shadows and death? The Lord didn't lead you there. You chose the darkness" [2]

Dr. Towns is correct to say that there are times when we do walk away from the Lord into the darkness and get ourselves into a mess. Such as, a man who is unfaithful to his wife, a college student who stops going to church, a woman who becomes bitter and stops praying after her sister dies. . . He/she suddenly wonders, "Why am I depressed? Why is my life a mess, right now?" The answer is probably because they wandered away from the Lord.

However, there are times when God leads us in a valley to test us and to grow our faith in Him, such as financial difficulties, illness, and other problems that often pop up when we are walking closely with God and serving Him with all our hearts. A shepherd, many times, would lead the sheep through the valleys to get to the bountiful fields on the other side of the hills. Albert Barnes says it so very well,

God will lead and guide me in the path of righteousness, even though that path lies through the darkest and most gloomy vale - through deep and dismal shades - in regions where there is no light, as if death had cast his dark and baleful shadow there. It is still a right path; it is a path of safety; and it will conduct me to bright regions beyond.[3]

The valleys through the mountains were the only way that the shepherd could get the sheep through the hills because of the sheep's physical makeup, as they could not climb the steep cliffs like the goats could. As with the Christian life, many times, the valleys are the only means by which God can perform His purposes in our lives. So consequently, we are either coming out of a valley, living in a valley, or going into a valley.

> **The valleys that are allowed in our lives are a part of God's working and purposes in our lives.**

The valleys that are allowed in our lives are a part of God's working and purposes in our lives, as He describes in the book of Job, "Yet man is born unto trouble, as the sparks fly upward" (Job 5:7). For the unsaved, the valley could be allowed to bring them to salvation, and for the saved, the valley is to bring them closer to Christ, where the great blessings are.

Unfortunately, in modern Christianity, we have fallen for the idea that once we accept Jesus, we can expect life to play out like a trip to the day spa. You hear statements like, "Jesus is our homey," and "Jesus is my buddy," or the application of Jesus being like a genie in a bottle, that if we rub Him the right way, we can get some wishes answered. I have heard some prosperity preachers teach that as soon as one gets saved, God is going to pour out spiritual blessings upon your life and you will be happy and jolly like never before, and you will be driving a new Cadillac. However, those of us who have been Christians for any length of time know this is misleading because so many Scriptures speak of suffering after you get saved. Like in John 15:18, "If the world hate you, ye know that it hated me before it hated you," and in 2 Timothy 3:12, "Yea, and all that will live godly in Christ Jesus shall suffer persecution."

One day, while listening to a local radio program, I heard the speaker say something that illustrates this point, "You know, in America, we preach this jolly Jesus. This jolly Jesus is so good and so happy, and a jolly good fellow, and if you just accept Jesus, this jolly good fellow, then you can be jolly too." He went on to say, "If you take this jolly Jesus of America to the Sudan, they would not even know who you are talking about because since they got saved, it's been persecution. They have seen their brothers, sisters, and children killed for Christ's sake, for taking a stand for God."

> We trust in the Lord, and leave all the particulars up to Him.

We, as Christians in a relationship with the Great Shepherd, must find our completeness in our Saviour and Shepherd. He has given us power in life and happiness in Him to live a joyful life in spite of the circumstances. That is one of the benefits of being a sheep in the fold of the Shepherd. We trust in the Lord and leave all the particulars up to Him. Romans 6:18 explains this trust, "Being then made free from sin, ye became the servants of righteousness." We serve a great Lord, and we are His servants of righteousness. Pastor Dewey Weaver, retired pastor of Gateway Baptist Church in Luster's Gate, Virginia, used to have a saying something like this, "Happiness is living a life, in the favor of the Saviour." Let us never charge our great Lord for not providing a *made to order* life, built around our often selfish desires.

So, yes, we can expect valleys, and they are in the economy of our relationship with our Shepherd. Valleys are a part of life for all humans. The unsaved go through deep valleys just like us. "That ye may be the children of your Father which is in heaven: for he maketh his sun to rise on the evil and on the good, and sendeth rain on the just and on the unjust" (Matthew 5:45).

The difference between their valleys and our valleys is that we have someone to walk with us, giving us hope of victory through them. The unsaved with no shepherd get in a valley and cannot cope. They have no one to look to, other than themselves and other tangible things. The unsaved often turn to drugs, to drinking, and/or require help from a therapist or psychiatrist. Without a relationship with the Almighty Physician, they are quick to turn to prescriptions as the cure for their pain and confusion.

> You and I, who are saved and know the Lord, know Who to turn to when we get in a valley. We look up to Jesus Christ.

A drawback with the movement of psychology is that some people tend to use psychology as an alternative to dealing with life without the Great Shepherd. There's nothing wrong with getting counseling, as long as the counselor directs the counselee to the Cross for healing. God created man and allows things in our lives, and He is the One Who can sustain us. You and I, who are saved and know the Lord, know Who to turn to when we get in the valley. We look up to Jesus Christ. Our responses as sheep of the Great Shepherd should be different than that of wild sheep of the world. This is the distinction I was talking about earlier.

Consequently, though we are Christians, this does not guarantee that we will still make the right decisions in the valley and look to the Great Shepherd. There are Christians whose lives are shipwrecked from not trusting in the Lord in the valley. We don't often recognize that our shipwrecked state came from not trusting the Lord. Sometimes we get so caught up in the circumstances that we don't even realize or pay attention to what has shipwrecked us. It takes awhile to see that we are going on knee-jerk reactions and panic mode, instead of taking time to seek and trust God. When I look at many bad decisions that people make, I can pinpoint that the problem is often, though they are saved, they feel like, "God's not gonna come through," or some will even say, "God's not going to take care of the situation." Some have even asked, "Where are you God?" Many may not even *verbally* say it; however, in their actions, that is exactly what they are saying and doing because they fail to trust in God.

Look at the last part of verse number four. The Psalmist says, "I will fear no evil." God is stating that we can be in that valley of the shadow of death without being fearful. Why? "Thou art with me." If we know that God is with us, it changes everything. I have said, so many times, that if we really believe that God is with us every single second, it would revolutionize the way we act and talk.

For example, as a pastor, I visit people all the time. I will come to visit someone, arrive at the door, and I will hear from the outside of the door, "Hey, the preacher's here!" Those inside will have televisions, radios, and computers turning off; not counting all of the magazines and other things being thrown under couches. Now, think about it with me. Forget about me, the preacher, being there at the door. The Lord Jesus Christ was there before I came! He saw everything! The fact is, the presence of God being right there with

His children should drive all of us to clean up our act and keep us trusting and looking to Him.

Likewise for us all, when we are in a constant state of God's presence in our lives as sheep, whether it is in the valleys or on the mountain tops, it will drive us to an introspective life. This is a critical point because we see that physical sheep have no way of protecting themselves, that they do not have sharp teeth or claws as a means to protect themselves, and the result for the sheep is, many times, they are driven by fear without a Shepherd. That is why they can be timid. David says in essence, as God's sheep, "I know that God is with me. I will fear no evil." Look what he says next: "Thy rod and Thy staff they comfort me." The rod and staff let the sheep know that the Shepherd is still with them.

The rod that is spoken of here, typically, is in the context of a punishing instrument that was traditionally used for the correction of children. The Bible says clearly about its use, "Thou shalt beat him with a rod, thou shalt deliver his soul from hell" (Proverbs 23:14). The Bible also states, "Withhold not correction from a child. If thou beatest him with a rod, he shall not die" (Proverbs 23:13).

Like so many of us when we were children, we remember the pain associated with getting a whipping. However, we look back at our childhood and see that it was probably for our good. Now think with me. Why must we discipline our children? Why does God command us to physically punish our children? The fact is that we must teach children boundaries. We discipline our children, teaching them that there is a right way, and there is a wrong way; there is a right reaction, and there is a wrong reaction. We teach them these things so that they will not get hurt later.

God promises a benefit to His discipline in Hebrews 12:7, "If ye endure chastening, God dealeth with you as with sons; for what son is he whom the father chasteneth not?" This coincides with our text, "The LORD is my shepherd...Yea, though I walk through the valley of the shadow of death, I will fear no evil: for thou art with me; thy rod and thy staff they comfort me" (Psalm 23).

Let's go back to our illustration. Here is the shepherd and the sheep in a valley. All of a sudden, the sheep are wandering away from the shepherd in the wrong direction. Maybe it is near a wolf pack, or maybe it is by a cliff. The shepherd will walk over with his staff, smite them, and say, "Hey, you have gotten out of bounds. You're not walking correctly. You're not walking in the right path (righteousness). The way you are walking is dangerous and not my will for you." The sheep then move away from the danger. The shepherd does this because he loves them and wants to protect them.

The rod here is also very comforting to the sheep because of the protection it represents. In the book, *The Lord Is My Shepherd*, by Greg Olson, he says,

> To the defenseless sheep, nothing is more comforting than to see the shepherd equipped with his rod and his staff. The rod was a heavy club, measuring two to three feet in length and the staff is a slender stick about eight feet along…The rod…denotes that the shepherd is concerned and capable of destroying any enemy… Whether the attacker be a wolf, coyote, or snake. [4]

The promise here, and the main subject I am writing about is, *How to Walk Through the Valleys of Life*. As we journey through life and valleys, we will want to stray from the Shepherd, thinking that we can lead our own way. I stated earlier that valleys leave us more vulnerable to bad decision-making. If we trust or look to anyone other than the Great Shepherd, the Lord Jesus Christ, we will fear, and this fear will drive us to make our lives a mess outside of the will of God.

The Shepherd and sheep relationship, as promised in Psalms 23:1-3, drives us through the valley victoriously. I know many Christians who used to serve God faithfully but no longer do. What happened? A valley came, and they could cope with it for a couple of weeks (we all have enough fleshly fortitude to get through a few weeks); however, in a prolonged valley, they looked to themselves or something else, and they seemly only got deeper in the valley and lost hope.

During the life of Job, for many years, it was as bad as it could have been for him. He lost family, friends, had severe health problems, financial problems, marriage problems, and topping all that off, he suffered much loneliness. What if that had been you? How could you continue to look to the Lord and trust Him like Job did?

What is your valley? What has you by the throat wondering how you'll continue? How will you continue? You may even be asking, "How in the world can I hang on another day?" Maybe you are saying, "I trusted the Lord, but I am exhausted; it is best that I give up." Please do not give up. Just keep reading.

The Purpose

One of the greatest helps for you in the valley is to realize that the trials of life have a purpose and divine approval. The general purpose is righteousness or right living as we follow the Shepherd, but the valley also has the purpose of a means to building our faith in the Lord. The Bible declares, "...without faith it is impossible to please God" (Heb 11:6).

Faith feeds our relationship with the Lord/Shepherd. Faith will enable us to keep looking and listening to the truth of the Shepherd and sheep relationship through all of our various valleys, in spite of the darkness that surrounds us. Faith will not allow us to say when the valley comes, "Why is this happening to me? Lord, I've been TRYING to be faithful to you!" "God, I've been GOING to church, READING my Bible and PRAYING, and look what's come into my life!" But faith will enable us to look to the Lord with unshakable trust.

> **Our faith must be tested to prove its ability to be trusted.**

The reason faith produces this kind of response in our lives is because our faith is the evidence of those things not seen. This faith looks to the person of Christ in the valley and not to the shadows in the depth of the valley. Faith is the response of our hearts to the character of the Shepherd.

Faith will enable us to look at the valley, and speak to the Lord, and say, "This valley, Lord, You have allowed it, You are my Shepherd, I am going to keep my eyes on You, and I will fear not, but I will have faith." Now, imagine with me that this had been your response in every situation you had ever dealt with in life. How would life be different today? What if you apply this thinking to the valley you're in now?

I have learned in my personal life, that my faith grows the most in the valleys. To respond wrongly, would be to miss many, and, if not most, of the valuable lessons in life. With faith being such a valuable asset, this faith must be exercised and tested; if not, then faith cannot be trusted. Just like all power tools on the market today, they are tested to ensure that they are safe to be used. Likewise, our faith must be tested to prove its ability to be trusted.

Now, remember, valleys are only a "shadow of death," and it is not speaking so much of a literal death. Keeping this idea in mind, valleys will produce lasting wisdom and righteousness in my life, for it keeps my mind stayed on a right outcome.

> **God will not use a man until He breaks him.**

However, do not be alarmed if, in these valleys of life, things hurt a little along the way. Righteousness and the lessons of life will always have a little hurt in them. God will not use a man until He breaks him. Just like a horse has to be broken before it can be used, so is man in his natural state.

To make this a little personal, during the writing of this book, I had a great valley come through my life. My wife and I were asleep one morning, and the phone rang about 5:30 a.m. The voice on the other side of the phone said, "Jerry, your mother passed away last night in her sleep." Now, this is a common experience for many, but for each one, the pain and emotions are different. To give you a brief background into my situation and loss, from the time I came to know the Lord as my Saviour, I tried to reach my mother for the Lord. She had several addictions and health problems that made her life hard. My wife and I, for years, flew her from her country home in Virginia to our home in Wisconsin to help her and get her health back in order, but she would always go back to her old ways. This went on for seven years with dozens of close calls and many attempts to counsel, encourage, rebuke, and love.

When I received the call, it was like a load of bricks were dumped in my stomach. From that loss, I was changed. I was changed in that it has made me a much better pastor and counselor. I know now, and, can visualize the pain of the people that I am ministering to. God used the death of my mother to break into my emotions, to teach me, and to help and heal me, so that I can help others. When situations come into our lives, He is producing a purpose in our lives.

When we look at Psalm 23:5 "...thou anointest my head with oil..." This verse implies that though we will get hurt by the thorns and

> **The Lord will allow pain in our lives, but He, Himself, will not harm us; and there is a big difference.**

thistles of life, and, at times, when we are disobedient to God, He has to smite us; our Shepherd will turn around and heal us too. The Lord will allow pain in our lives, but He, Himself, will not harm us; and there is a big difference.

The kind of hurt is like this: if your appendix became inflamed today, you would be rushed to a doctor, and the doctor would send you into surgery. The doctor would hurt you when he cut into your body, but he would not harm you. The word harm is indicative of permanent damage. When the surgery is all over, he would have helped you by saving your life, by removing your appendix.

Just like the medical doctor, the Shepherd will allow hurt, and He will even hurt you at times. However, He will not harm you, but will have helped you when all things are said and done. Just like Solomon says in Ecclesiastes 7:3, "Sorrow is better than laughter: for by the sadness of the countenance the heart is made better." How have your past or present valleys hurt you? Though the valleys may hurt, you'll be better off in the end, though it may be hard to understand presently.

Without valleys in our lives for His purposes, we can never be what God wants us to be. That is why God says that those who will live Godly shall suffer persecution (2 Tim 3:12). Persecution is where character is born and where more love and appreciation for our Lord Jesus Christ is attained. As 1 Peter 1:7 says, "That the trial of your faith, being much more precious than of gold that perisheth, though it be tried with fire, might be found unto praise and honour and glory at the appearing of Jesus Christ:" However, in the midst of that valley, many times, as we have already stated, we forget that God is with us, which means we have lost our faith in the Lord.

The same is true of stubborn habits that we struggle with in life. It seems like, when one gets saved, God takes away many of the struggles at that time. He leaves some things in our lives that we continue to struggle with, such as bitterness, or lying, but at the same time, He may give us complete victory over other struggles, such as drinking alcohol. For years, this concept puzzled me. I kept asking myself, "If God is so concerned that I live right, why did He not choose, in His supernatural power, to deliver me from all sin?" I believe the answer to this is that if we did not have some sin and struggles to deal with through the

Persecution is where character is born.

Lord, how would we ever learn to trust Him? God leaves some sins and situations in our lives that need to be worked out only through Him. I believe that is why when the disciples could not cast out a demon automatically, Jesus told them in Matthew 17:21, "Howbeit this kind goeth not out but by prayer and fasting." So, the pain or sin that we are struggling with has been left for us to work out through the Lord, and it has a definite purpose and goal. God has left it to help us trust in Him or to build a particular area of our lives.

Let us say that the valley is a financial valley. You have lost your job, bills come in unexpectedly, and you react wrongly by fearing, and say, "Well, I cannot give to God anymore. You know, I can use this money for something else." Unfortunately, rather than going through the valley, we get deeper in the valley. The valley becomes a ditch of the Devil rather than a valley from the Lord to be used. Dr. Lee Robertson used to say all the time, "A rut is a grave with both ends knocked out." So when we get in the midst of a financial valley and say, "I can't give to God anymore," and we stop giving, we forget that God is with us and that God is still the Shepherd. But the same God that I served before the valley is the same God during the valley.

One day, I was talking to a preacher with an earned doctorate and a good resume of ministry. This servant of the Lord had been to Bible College and Seminary. He probably knows more about the Bible than I do. His story goes that his little girl died. Then his life went to shambles. He relayed this story to me. He said, "I grew up in a home where there was casual drinking; taking a little drink now and then was not that bad. I got in this deep valley, and I turned to drinking to ease my pain." He looked to the booze to get him through the valley, even though he knew a lot about the Lord.

His education in the Lord didn't make any difference when he got in the valley. His little girl died, and he pondered and pondered in the valley. He had to face the facts that for the rest of his life, he would have to deal with the reality that his little girl was never coming home, and that he would never hold his little girl in his arms again. He went to the booze bottle, got addicted, and lost everything as far as his ministry is concerned at that time. We will finish his story a little later.

Some would hear this story and say that this servant of the Lord should have known better, and that he should have been a stronger person. Often, we make the mistake of assuming that some people should be above falling or buckling under stress. I would say that we all as God's children should know better. This same situation can happen to us all if we fail to walk through the valley in faith with our eyes on the Lord, knowing that the pain will produce a harvest of fruit in our lives. Just remember that there can be no victory, unless there is opposition.

So let's review:

- God knows our needs and wants, and He has taken it as His job to provide for them.
- Life is full of valleys, and the valleys have a purpose.
- In order for the Lord to be our Shepherd, we must be saved and allow Him to lead us.
- Valleys are the places where our faith grows the most.
- Losing sight of the Lord will only mean that we will get deeper and worse off in the valley.

These truths will set the foundation for the rest of this book.

CHAPTER 2

THE VALLEY IS GOD'S HALLWAY

I looked ahead, and I saw a great sea. The water was deep, and the waves were deafening. I looked back, and the sound of hoofs and wagon wheels filled my ears, and my eyes were fixed on the rising dust as the great army approached. Everyone traveling with me cried, "What will we do?" Then God spoke and said, "Go forth!" So I stretched out the rod in my hand, and the waters parted. We crossed the sea on dry ground.

Moses
Exodus 14

Turning a Valley into a Hallway

The reality of walking through the valleys of life is one of the most integral attributes for us as Christians. Never should we be taken off guard by a valley in life, but we should always be expecting valleys to come and planning for them. A valley need not be looked at as a negative for our lives, but instead, a positive building block in the Christian's growth. However, a valley that has turned into a rut is always negative; thus it needs to be regarded as such. A rut, in this sense, is a valley in which we have lost hope. A rut will always take you places that you do not want to go. This wrong path is a walking away from the Lord.

In Virginia, where I grew up, we had a lot of dirt roads. During the month of April, we would have heavy rain, and the roads would wash out. The roads would be filled with ruts, and if you were driving and hit one, they would almost take you over the bank of the road, in the direction the water ran off the road. The reason the water runs over to the side of the road is that water always flows to the easiest path of resistance and to the lowest lying areas, which is mostly to the side of the road in the ditch. Needless to say, over the bank is not where we need to be. We need to stay on the road.

When the valleys come in our lives, we cannot let the ruts (valleys) dictate our path, but instead, let the purposes of the Lord lead us. Like water which flows to the easiest paths of resistance, we, as Christians, gravitate to the path that has the least resistance. We are like natural sheep; they like things easy. If the path is easy, immediately, one would wonder if this was the right path from the Lord.

Often I will hear Christians say, "If the Lord opens the doors, then I will go." When we say, "If the Lord opens the doors," we are prone to get lazy and sit back waiting for something to fall in our lap. "God didn't open the door," becomes our excuse for staying where we are. However, what needs to be said is, "Lord I am going to go at Your command, and trust that You will open the doors." This thinking will take what seems to be a rut or negative valley and turn it into a hallway for the Lord, letting God's purposes keep us in the middle of the valley's path, and ultimately, leading us to a greater faith in the Lord.

The way you prepare and plan to turn your valley into a hallway that God can use is by seeing the valleys as opportunities for God

| Valleys are many, but the solution is the same. |

to use in some way; thus making up your mind to be victorious in those valleys, no matter what they may be. I hear so many people say, "You don't know what I am going through." "You can't feel all my pain." Listen, the various valleys are not as important as the solution. Valleys are many, but the solution is the same. Being victorious does not mean denying that the valley hurts or is difficult. It just means not letting it consume us or bring out our worst.

That is why 2 Timothy 1:7 says, "For God hath not given us the spirit of fear; but of power, and of love, and of a sound mind." Remember the promise from Psalm 23, "I will fear no evil." Thus, you need to "cast your burden upon Him." God promises He will carry the burden for you. That means, during one's loneliness, financial problems, grief, guilt, reaping of wickedness, marriage problems, and joblessness, He will work in and through them, and walk with you during them if you will trust in Him and commit your life to Him; thus making this valley a hallway that God can use.

The greatest valley that we as Christians have come through is the valley of sin. Think of it this way: if God can take care of our deepest, ugliest sin, then He will have no problem taking care of our other problems. If you are reading this, and you are not saved, you obviously are going through the valley of sin. This valley has been there all of your life and will eventually destroy you. The only way that you are going to get out of this valley is to trust Jesus as your personal Saviour. If you do not get out of the rut of sin, you will end up in eternity without Christ. Forward to Chapter Eight and read the section "How to Come Into the Fold and Get Identity with the Shepherd," and take care of this step right now, before continuing.

Don't Run

Remember when you were in school? You would run down the hall, and the teacher would stop you and say, "Where's the fire? You do not need to run, we are here all day." Then she would say something like this, "Slow down and be safe."

This illustration is perfect for us as we walk in these valley hallways of our lives. We fail many times to walk through the valley because we are actually trying to run out of it. We get in a hurry for

no reason. We are in the valley for the unknown duration, whether
we like it or not. To run in the valley is
just as dangerous as not even looking to
the Great Shepherd in the valley.

**We fail many times
to walk through the
valley because we are
actually trying to run
out of it.**

We have a tendency to run away, or
in other words, try to escape the valley
because we think that running away will
relieve us from the pain of the situation.
Some of the pain associated with the
valley is part of the program, and running only makes it worse for
us. Have you ever seen firewalkers? I think they would be better
named fire runners. They run across the coals, and the heat does
not have time to burn through the bottoms of their feet. They really
do not impress me that much. What would be amazing to me is if
they walked slowly, or that they stopped for a minute and were not
burned. Have you been guilty of wanting to run out of your valleys
before God's plan can be revealed and worked in your life?

When Christians walk through the valley slowly, trusting in
the Lord's care, everything in life then works on the Lord's timing,
instead of the circumstances at hand. The Lord says in Isaiah 43:2,
"When thou passest through the waters, I will be with thee; and
through the rivers, they shall not overflow thee: when thou walkest
through the fire, thou shalt not be burned; neither shall the flame
kindle upon thee." What a great promise for us as Christians!

Notice that the verse says that we "will not be burned." It does
not say that the fire will not get a little hot on our feet. In the valley,
we tend to take off running as soon as we feel a little heat under
our feet. However, faith tells us that we will not be burned. The
three Hebrew children, in the book of Daniel, had the faith to march
right into the fiery furnace. God was with them and they were not
burned.

I do not know about you, but if I am in pain, I want instant
relief; it's natural. My wife is the exact opposite. If she has a
toothache or a headache, she does not take medicine. She deals
with the pain. If I have a headache, or a sore toe, or an ingrown
toenail, give me about five aspirins and call me in the morning. I
do not want to deal with the pain at all. Pain in life reveals to us
God's working. Just like a fever, many times, shows that there is
a physical problem that should not be ignored, neither does the
pain in the valley need to be avoided. Instead, it can be dealt with

through the Lord. Those seeking instant relief in a valley miss much of what God is doing in the valley.

Charles Spurgeon wrote:

> The path of the Christian is not always bright with sunshine; he has his seasons of darkness and of storm. True, it is written in God's Word," her ways are ways of pleasantness, and all her paths are peace;" and it is a great truth, that religion is calculated to give a man happiness below as well as bliss above; but experience tells us that if the course of the just be "As the shining light that shineth more and more unto the perfect day," yet sometimes *that* light is eclipsed. At certain periods clouds cover the believer's sun, and he walks in darkness and sees no light........they have walked along the 'green pastures' by the side of the 'still waters,' but suddenly they find the glorious sky is clouded; instead of the Land of Goshen they have to tread the sandy desert; in the place of sweet waters, they find troubled streams, bitter to their taste, and they say, Surely, if I were a child of God, this would not happen.' Oh! say not so, thou who art walking in darkness. The best of God's saints must drink the wormwood; the dearest of His children must bear the cross. No Christian has enjoyed perpetual prosperity;[5]

Just like a lady who becomes pregnant, for nine months her body is changing, organs are shifted, and an extra 30-50 pounds are carried. Then, the delivery comes. Being there, myself, for the birth of all four of our boys, I know that the woman goes through a pain likened unto death. But as soon as the baby is born, the pain and the hurt are no longer of importance. A precious child has been brought into the world. As we have been born again, we also have some pain associated with being sanctified with the Lord, but the finished product is great.

> Can two walk together except they be agreed?
> Amos 3:3

The pain that comes in the valley is allowed by our Shepherd, Who is guiding us. When we run in God's hallway, we are actually running from God rather than from the pain. We aren't usually aware of what we are running from. So as we enter the valley, we need to stop, ponder, and claim the promise of Isaiah 40:31, which says, "They that wait upon the LORD shall renew their strength; they shall mount up with wings as eagles; they shall run and not be weary; and they shall walk, and not faint."

As God allows valleys/hallways in life, our perspective needs to be that we will just stand back and do as Psalm 27:14 says, "Wait on the Lord: be of good courage." Wait and walk with God during those times while letting God's full plan be unfolded in His timing. The valley will be more enjoyable from this approach.

As the Word of God says, "Can two walk together except they be agreed" (Amos 3:3)? If we are walking through the valley with the Lord, we will be in step and stride with the One Who has allowed this in our lives. Our Shepherd, at times, will carry us if the situation calls for it.

God is in no hurry. He already knows the beginning and the end. As we walk with Him, if we take off running, we end up leading Him rather than Him leading us.

Those with little children will know exactly what I am talking about. If you take your kids to a store, say for example, Wal-Mart, even though you may be the parent, the kids start to lead. The kids get rambunctious and start pulling you through the store because they are so eager to get to the next toy. As sheep of the Shepherd, we act like children in a store. We get in the valleys and say, "No, God. Let me go. Let me out of here. I know what I want, and You just need to get out of my way so I can get it. You're hindering me from attaining what I need in my life." We, as God's children, never benefit from this attitude, for we have to trust the Lord and make sure that He is leading instead of us leading Him.

These valleys in our lives have important lessons attached to them that God is trying to show us, and these same lessons will take time to learn. Again, 1 Peter 1:7 says, "That the trial of your faith, being much more precious than of gold that perisheth, though it be tried with fire, might be found unto praise and honor and glory at the appearing of Jesus Christ:"

When we are in the valleys of life, we would like nothing more than to avoid the pain and the darkness of the valleys, but in reality, if we were to miss the pain and darkness, we would not appreciate the light as much, once we turn our valley into a hallway and walk through it. As God promises to be with us in our lives, He promises a safe landing, but He does not promise a calm passage. "Surely goodness and mercy shall follow me all the days of my life: and I will dwell in the house of the LORD forever" (Psalms 23:6).

Parking and Pouting

Running in God's hallway is not the only problem when walking through the valleys. Some people do what I call parking and pouting. Some say, "God, I'm depressed, so I am not going to do anything or go anywhere!" They use the valley as an excuse to justify complacency. They find solace in just sitting and complaining about their circumstances rather than walking through them.

This reminds me of a story from out west. A cowboy was driving down a dirt road. His dog was riding in the back of the pickup truck, and his faithful horse was in the trailer behind. The cowboy failed to negotiate a curve and had a terrible accident. Sometime later, a highway patrol officer came on the scene. The officer, being an animal lover, saw the horse first. Realizing the serious nature of its injuries, he drew his service revolver and put the animal out of his misery. He walked around the accident and found the dog, also hurt critically. He couldn't bear to hear the dog whine in pain, so he ended the dog's suffering as well.

Finally, he located the cowboy off in the weeds. He had suffered multiple fractures. The man asked the cowboy, "Hey, are you okay?" The cowboy took one look at the smoking revolver in the trooper's hand and quickly replied, "Never felt better!"

The moral to this story is that we need to be careful about complaining in the valley because when we park and pout, the valley only gets worse. The cowboy did not want to deal with the supposed circumstances of the complaining; thus all of a sudden his wounds did not hurt. There was great condemnation poured out from the Heavenly Father upon His people when they complained.

> **Remember, we also have an enemy called Satan, who can also use the valley, if we let him.**

Think back when the nation of Israel complained about the wilderness, the food, the water, and God's guidance. Consequently, God dealt with them severely, sending serpents and making examples out of some people when they complained. We, likewise, will have consequences if we park and pout in the valley. Being complacent and stagnant is just as destructive as running through God's hallway. As you analyze your life, have you been guilty of parking and pouting in your various valleys? Any activity other than God's directed plan is ineffective. Some people have asked me, "Why do you have so much energy? Why do you have so much enthusiasm? Why do you preach every message like it is your last?" I usually respond by saying that I would rather burn out than rust out. I never want to go out on a dud. Likewise, I never want to be caught by the Lord parking and pouting about His working in my life.

Remember, we also have an enemy called Satan, who can also use the valley if we let him. When Satan sees us parking and pouting, he says, "Now I've GOT 'EM!" Literally, we become a sitting duck in the sights of the Devil (1 Peter 5:8). "Be sober, be vigilant; because your adversary the devil, as a roaring lion, walketh about, seeking whom he may devour:" When we fail to walk through the valley, Satan gets his gun out and tries to put us out of our misery.

We are the salt of the earth, the Bible states. When we get complacent in the valley, we risk losing our salt savor. This salt comparison is very interesting when it comes to the Christian life. An illustration of the way we are to preserve and keep walking through the valley is found in the process of making a salt/sugar-cured ham.

A salt/sugar-cured ham does not have to be refrigerated. After a little studying on the subject, one finds out that the people who prepare the ham just put a lot of brown sugar and salt on the meat. The salt rub absorbs in the ham. Then, after a day or so of having that salt and sugar solution on the ham, you will hear a sizzling-type noise, almost like it is frying. However, there is no heat! The salt is a preservative. The ham gets its preservative this way, and once salt gets into that fresh meat, it is like pouring salt into a wound. It creates a hostile environment. The salt keeps the cells moving. As long as the salt keeps the cells moving in and on the meat, the bacteria cannot stick to it; thus, the meat is then preserved for many years.

Bacteria and algae need a complacent environment to grow. Green ponds are a result of water not moving. If you have a fish aquarium, you know that if you keep the water moving, the water stays fresh longer. When we sit during a valley, we get complacent, and the algae from Satan will get all over us, and it is a downhill spiral from there.

The over all picture here is, when you are walking through the valley/hallway, you have to determine that no matter what, you are going to go through the valley by keeping on the way of the Lord. I am going forward for the Lord as Hebrews 12:1-2 commands:

> Wherefore seeing we also are compassed about with so great a cloud of witnesses, let us lay aside every weight, and the sin which doth so easily beset us, and let us run with patience the race that is set before us, Looking unto Jesus the author and finisher of our faith; who for the joy that was set before him endured the cross, despising the shame, and is set down at the right hand of the throne of God.

Jesus Christ was our example of how to go through the valley by keeping our eyes on the Lord and His purpose for humanity. The joy that was set before Him was God's plan for salvation.

I do not know what you have been through, are going through today, or what you may face tomorrow. One universal fact is, *I am going to have to keep continuing through the valley; I am not getting out of the valley, and I am going to be here until the purpose of God is fulfilled in my life; until God chooses either to deliver me, or I learn all the things God wants to show me.*

With this determination, I dedicate that I am staying right here. I am going to make the best of it for God and let God make the best of it for me. A preacher, named Dr. Jack Hyles, used to say that he took all of his dictionaries in his office and cut the word "quit" out of them because he hated the word so much. Now, I don't know if we need to go to that extreme or not, but I know we need to remove the action of quitting, parking, and pouting out of our lives.

CHAPTER 3

THE LIGHT AT THE END OF THE TUNNEL

"But as for you, ye thought evil against me; but God meant it unto good, to bring to pass, as it is this day, to save much people alive."

Joseph
Genesis 50:20

"When you feel a valley coming on, have no fear, God's light is near." Patricia Ann Williams (my mother)

God's Divine Outcome

When I was growing up in the hills of Virginia, I loved to explore places, especially caverns. It just so happens that there are many caves near my childhood home. One time, my cousin and I were exploring a cave, and the flashlight that we brought with us went out several hundred feet inside the cave. At that moment, we were in complete darkness, and I got very nervous. We frantically crawled on our hands and knees trying to retrace our path, but it seemed to be hopeless. Then off in the distance, I could see a little pin hole of a light. In desperation, we made our way to the light the best way we knew how. The closer we got to the light, the larger it appeared, and the more we could see. It was the opening to the cave.

In the darkness of life's valleys, it is easy for us to lose our way and be overcome by the shadows of darkness. We forget God's purposes and who we are as His Sheep. Being overcome by darkness will cause us to lose sight and direction, thus, making us panic and feel out of control. Now, back to the illustration: as soon as I realized for sure that what I was seeing was the opening of the cave, and it was not just my imagination, the panic left me. Likewise, our walk through the valleys should be the same way. No matter how dark it gets, there is always a light at the end of the tunnel. We know that the Lord is in control in the valley, and that there will be a divine outcome. This divine outcome is the light at the end of the tunnel.

> **We must keep in mind that no matter how dark it gets, God is still with us.**

The Darkness

As a child, I was afraid of the dark because I thought that somewhere in the shadows of the night there were monsters. Though I had never seen a monster personally, I was thoroughly convinced of their existence. There were two things that eased my fears of dark nights.

First, I wanted my mother and/or father to come into my room and stay with me. I believed that if there really were monsters, the monsters would be afraid of my parents, and I would be protected.

We, as Christians, are God's sheep, and we must keep in mind that no matter how dark it gets, God is still with us, for He never leaves us. God gives us this promise in Hebrews 13:5b, "...for he hath said, I will never leave thee, nor forsake thee," and in Psalms 121:4, "Behold, he that keepeth Israel shall neither slumber nor sleep." Your Daddy has never left you in the valley, and He never will. He is right there with you all the way.

Nighttime was a very dangerous time for the natural sheep in the fold. It was dangerous because the sheep would bed down at night in the open fields and valleys in the country. This would be the time when many of their predators would attack. If at all possible, the shepherd would often try to find a cave, and bed down at nights for their protection. This cave, typically, would only have one opening, and the sheep would be herded into the cave. Then, the shepherd would sleep prostrate in the opening of the cave. If the sheep tried to stray out, or if the predators tried to come in, they would have to pass by the shepherd. Jesus assures us in John 10:7, "... Verily, verily, I say unto you, I am the door of the sheep." Just like the natural shepherd is the doorkeeper for the natural sheep, Jesus (our Shepherd) is the doorkeeper of our lives, and nothing gets to us, unless it comes through Him first.

> **My outlook on life changed, when the light came on!**

The sheep in this dark cave would know that the shepherd had the door covered for their protection. Likewise, you and I have that same assurance that God is with us and that no matter how dark it gets, His light is shining bright; thus, all we have to do is look for it.

The second thing that helped me in the darkness was to turn on the light in my room. Once it was on, I was no longer scared. In the dark valleys of life, we have a light from our Lord that needs to be turned on. That light is God's divine outcome. God has proved Himself to us in the valley and in the fields, so no matter how dark it gets, God is still with us. A classic statement I heard in a sermon one time is, "Never doubt in the darkness what God has shown you in the light."

The problem, however, is that we find that the light is hard to turn on in the darkness of our lives. Just like when Jesus came to earth to die for the sins of humanity, the men and women of the earth, at that time, did not even recognize Him. "And the light shineth in darkness; and the darkness comprehended it not" (John 1:5). These people were walking side-by-side with Jesus, and they did not even know it. Today, many times, the Lord is with us, and, we, as God's children, don't even recognize it. We must open our eyes to comprehend the light in our dark valley and flick on the switch that God has for us, so that we might see His divine outcome in our valley. As Jesus stated, "Then spake Jesus again unto them, saying, I am the light of the world: he that followeth me shall not walk in darkness, but shall have the light of life" (John 8:12).

When we consider God's purpose and outcome together, this is the flicking on of the switch. I don't know about you, but there have been times in my life when I was going through something, and all of a sudden the light came on, and it was very apparent why I was going through the problem. My outlook on life changed when the light came on!

This flicking on of the switch reminds me when I was back in grade school, taking tests and passing school grades. A child needs to pass the majority of his tests to show that he has learned the material. The goal is always to pass and understand the subject. No good teacher looks to purposely fail their students, but he/she works hard, with every means possible, to get the child to retain the information. However, when a child fails a grade, it is usually said to the child, "You have not learned in this grade all the things that you needed to learn; therefore, you cannot go onto the next grade. You must repeat a year; so that you can master all the information taught in this grade, in order to be prepared to move up to the next grade."

> **The path of the just is as the shining light, that shineth more and more unto the perfect day.**
> **Proverbs 4:18**

This same approach happens to us spiritually when the trials, tests, and valleys come. Until we get the information or lesson from the valley, we will keep retaking the same test. Many times, Christians live in this vicious cycle of continuing to take tests and going through valleys over and over again, frantically scurrying about rather than moving forward into the divine outcome. They end up like the nation of Israel, wandering in the wilderness rather than marching in the direction God would have them. The ironic thing about the nation of Israel's wanderings was that they were only miles from crossing the Jordan into the Promised Land, but they would not follow the Lord. So, the lesson that we need to learn is to find the light and go to it. Have you been guilty of continually taking the same tests over and over again in life?

> **Figuring out the purpose of the valley and its divine outcome makes the valleys of life a great adventure.**

God's specific purpose and outcome for the valleys are as the Bible states in Proverbs 4:18, "But the path of the just is as the shining light, that shineth more and more unto the perfect day." This light in the valley, though small in the beginning, will direct our steps, and the path will get brighter as we walk toward it.

The nation of Israel, after leaving Egypt, perfectly illustrates God's guidance and direction (Exodus chapters 13-14). Moses gets Joseph's bones and journeys out of Egypt to the Promised Land. God gave them a cloud by day and a fire by night to lead them.

The reason that God gave them this kind of guidance was because in Exodus 14, God had hardened the heart of Pharaoh, thus, moving Pharaoh to chase after the Israelites after he had let them go. This could have really discouraged the nation if God had not provided guidance. This cloud by day and fire by night kept Israel's focus forward to God's purpose in Canaan Land while being chased by Pharaoh's large army. The fire and cloud ahead kept the nation from looking back to the great army that was chasing them.

Figuring out the purpose of the valley and its divine outcome makes the valleys of life a great adventure. When we have the right perspective with our problems

> **ALL things work together for good.**

or valleys, we will head toward the divine outcome bravely. This dynamic truth of God's divine outcome in every situation changes the initial shock value of the tragedies that pop up in our lives. As you read this, and your valley seems dark and deep, I want to remind you that there is a light, and the light should really stand out in the darkness of your valley. You just need to focus and go toward it.

Think about the life of Job, and how he walked through the valley of the shadow of death and feared no evil, and God kept him.

We look back with hindsight, and we see the big picture in Job's life, and rejoice in his victory; but he did not have the same advantage as we have today. Job only knew that he was going through the valley, that God was with him, and that God was going to work it all out in the end. Job 19:25 says, "For I know that my redeemer liveth, and that he shall stand at the latter day upon the earth:" God can keep you just as he kept Job. Job knew this, and that is why he stated, "Though he slay me, yet will I trust in Him" (Job 13:15). (We will deal with the life of Job as an illustration more a little later.)

Like Job's example, we must determine that we are walking through the valley toward the light at the end of the tunnel and claim Romans 8:28, which says, very clearly, "And we know that all things work together for good to them that love God, to them who are the called according to his purpose."

If you love God and are called according to His purpose, the verse says that ALL things work together for good (divine outcome). That includes the bad, the good, the stressful, and the perplexing. I liken this, "that all things working together," to working a puzzle. If I am focused on a single piece but don't have the big picture in mind, I will never work the puzzle correctly. Though valleys seem to be perplexing to us, if we will work through the valley puzzle one piece at a time, keeping in mind the big picture (the light at the end of the tunnel), the valley will work itself out for God's glory and our good. The words of A. W. Tozer sum it up so well:

To the child of God, there is no such thing as an accident. He travels an appointed way. . . . Accidents may indeed appear to befall him and misfortune stalks his way; but these evils will be so in appearance only and will seem evils only because we cannot read the secret script of God's hidden providence.[6]

The Hope

The sheep in the sheepfold, as they went through the valleys, would fear because they felt trapped by the closed-in space between the mountains, scared of the possibility of being cornered by a wolf and unable to runaway to safety. Likewise, in the valley, they would not have such easy access to grass and food. The big pasture land was outside the valley. There were enough provisions to get them through the valley, but there were not enough provisions for them to survive in the valley, permanently. The sheep found solace in the fact that no matter how scary the situation appeared, they knew that there was a pasture somewhere at the end of the valley. The sheep knew that there was an end to the valley sooner or later, and that there were better provisions ahead.

> **If God led you in the valley, then He will lead you out.**

As Christians, this truth that the sheep realized brings about hope in our walk through our personal valleys. If God led you in the valley, then He will lead you out. An illustration of this is found in an experiment that I read about one day:

A number of years ago, researchers performed a study to see the effect that hope had on those undergoing hardship.

> Two sets of laboratory rats were placed in separate tubs of water. The researchers left one set in the water, and found that within an hour, they had all drowned. The other rats were periodically lifted out of the water and then returned. When that happened, the second set of rats swam for over 24 hours. Why? Not because they were given a rest, but because they suddenly had hope! Those animals somehow hoped that if they could stay afloat just a little longer, someone would reach down and rescue them. If hope holds such power for unthinking rodents, how much greater should its effect be on our lives. [7]

I pray that you have not lost hope, and that you will realize that God is holding you in the middle of your troubles.

The Focus of the Light

As we ascertain the light at the end of the tunnel, (the divine outcome) we need to note that God's divine outcome may have a slightly different focus, at times, in correlation with the outcome of our valley. Now, I know that the last statement I made may be a

> **The focuses will be a trial or test, a temptation, and/or chastisement from the Lord.**

little confusing. Let me explain: This focus is your interpretation of the purpose and outcome. The outcome is the same, but the lessons that are learned along the way may be different.

When you focus on something with your eyes, ample light is needed, which is the reason you cannot see in the dark. The light reflects off the object and your eyes process that light. The lens in your eye opens and closes, depending on how much light is needed to focus. If there is not enough light, then you strain your eyes trying to see. Did you ever notice that if the light is dim, you have to focus on the object for a few seconds in order for your eyes to see it clearly? Our hearts are our spiritual eyes, and these spiritual eyes must focus on the purpose and the outcome of the valleys, as well as the lessons learned; so that we make the right decisions, and these right decisions hinge upon having the right focus. When I use the word FOCUS, I mean the process of finding out how God is going to use this particular trouble my life, why He allowed it, and what are the lessons to be learned.

Likewise, as we focus on the light at the end of the tunnel, and we try to figure out where to go and how to respond, an important truth to know about the focus of the valley is that we need to fit it into one of these following three categories. The focuses will either be a trial/test, temptation, and/or chastisement from the Lord. All three of these categories have different responses; though they may have the same outcome. It is like this: let us say that a financial valley has come into your life. God may have allowed it as a test to see if you would be faithful to tithe to Him in spite of the financial strain. The purpose is

> **God will never lead you where grace cannot keep you.**

to build your faith in the Lord for financial provisions. The outcome is that God might eventually bless you financially and give you lots of money to finance His work on this earth. The focus is how you interpret the valley in your life, and this will dictate your response. If you interpret the valley as a temptation rather than a test from the Lord, your wrong interpretation of the valley could potentially make you miss a lot of the purpose and even the outcome for the valley. We are commanded to resist the Devil, so by interpreting this valley as a temptation, we, essentially, resist God's working and disregard the divine outcome that God willed to produce.

Let us think of it this way: if the valley that is allowed by the

Shepherd involves temptation from Satan (Now, remember, God will never lead us to sin, nor can He be tempted with evil, as He promises in James 1:13.), God allows the temptation because He knows we have the ability to be successful. He has already empowered us to get through it if we trust in Him (2 Peter 1:3). "According as his divine power hath given unto us all things that pertain unto life and godliness, through the knowledge of him that hath called us to glory and virtue:" As the promise goes, "God will never lead you where grace cannot keep you."

The purpose of our temptation is to resist Satan and draw close to God (James 4:7). "Submit yourselves therefore to God. Resist the devil, and he will flee from you." The divine outcome is a stronger assured faith. If we interpret the valley incorrectly as a test from the Lord, while it is really a temptation from Satan, then we are not guarded and resistant to Satan and his devices as much during the valley as we need to be. We are to submit to God and resist the Devil. These are completely different actions and focuses in the valley.

Let's suppose that God has brought a valley in our lives for the focused purpose of chastisement because of sin in our lives. The outcome of it is repentance. If we focus on this valley as either a test or a temptation, then, again, we may even miss the divine outcome. Proper focus in the valley is vitally important.

Looking back to the life of Job, God says about Job in chapter one, verse one, "There was a man in the land of Uz, whose name was Job; and that man was perfect and upright, and one that feared God, and eschewed evil," God says that Job was perfect, he was upright, and that he ran from evil. Think with me. How many times do we hear people say, "He did not deserve that!" or "Why do bad things happen to good people?" when they are trying to understand life's problems. In Job's life, here is a set of great perplexing situations that come upon Job for God's Glory. This was a test to show forth Job's character in the Lord.

As the story unfolds, Job had seven sons, three daughters, seven thousand sheep, three thousand camels, five hundred yolks of oxen, five hundred she-asses, and a great household. He was the greatest man of wealth in the east. Then Job's life takes a detour in Job 1:6-7:

> Now there was a day when the sons of God came to present themselves before the LORD, and Satan came also

among them. And the LORD said unto Satan, whence comest thou? Then Satan answered the LORD and said, From going to and fro in the earth, and from walking up and down in it.

Here is what is happening — (in my words)

Satan says, "I've been going to and fro," and, "I've been out trying to destroy people's lives and get some people in the valleys."

God says, "Have you considered my servant Job?"

Satan says, "No, I didn't because you're so good to him. There is no use trying. Your blessings are so great upon his life. He's got all these sheep, oxen, and he's got his great family and all these great things that are going on in his life. Why should I bother with him?"

Satan goes on to say, "God, let's see him in a valley, and we'll just see if he'll still serve you!"

God says (again in my words), "Okay, go ahead. You can see him in a valley."

So, a series of events happen to Job; but these trials do not arise because of anything he has done, personally. These trials are nothing more than tests to prove his unfeigned faith in the Lord. The end result was God's glory being shown through the life of Job still today, thousands of years later.

There's an important note here: the reason that Satan was kicked out of Heaven was that He wanted to take God's glory. In Job's life, God allowed trials to happen to show forth His glory through Job's faith in the valleys. The divine outcome was that God gave back to Job more than he started with and God was mightily magnified. Just like Jesus said about Lazarus, who was sick and eventually died, "When Jesus heard the news, he said, This sickness is not unto death, but for the glory of God, that the Son of God might be glorified thereby" (John 11:4).

Today, Satan has no new tricks. He attacks us as Christians just like he did Job. Satan wants to destroy *your* life. He wants to take God's glory from His children who are serving Him by getting them in a valley and turning their eyes off God. Satan wants God's children to miss the light and lose the focus that is going to guide us, so that the Lord would no longer be our Shepherd. If he can get us away from our Shepherd, then we are open game for him.

The God that I serve on the mountain top *is* my God of the valleys also. Reflect on one of those times when you quit in the valleys or at least wanted to. What actually happens is that you give up on God because you seemingly cannot figure out what He is doing. You no longer have the spiritual motivation to keep going, so you stop letting God work in and through your prayer life, Bible reading, and trust in Him. Then the unfortunate result is that you bring glory to Satan rather than God. Satan actually becomes your shepherd. As you think back when you have quit or wanted to, what if you had accepted that there was a purpose, and had seen a light at the end of the tunnel, and you had a fresh focus on the valley? Do you think your end result would have changed?

> The God that I serve on the mountain top *is* my God of the valleys also.

When we fail to see these truths, we are saying in essence, "Our God is the God of the hilltops, but He is not sufficient in the valleys." Why is this? It is because it seems to be easier for us to serve God on the mountain tops because we are normally getting what we want. (Even though a few Christians will quit on the mountaintops, most will quit in the valleys.) The God that I serve on the mountain top *is* my God of the valleys also. Romans 8:37 says, "Nay in all these things we are more than conquerors through him…" "Yea, though I walk through the valley of the shadow of death…for thou art with me" (Psalm 23). 1 Corinthians 10:13 says, "For there is no temptation taken you but such is as common to man: but God is faithful, who will not suffer you to be tempted above that ye are able; but will with the temptation also make a way to escape [walking through the valley]… that you may be able to bear it." Our Shepherd is faithful, no matter what the circumstances are, whether it is a valley or a mountain top.

Now, considering the divine outcome and God's showing us the light at the end of the tunnel, 1 Corinthians 10:13 is often misconstrued and taken out of context. "There hath no temptation taken you but such as is common to man: but God is faithful, who will not suffer you to be tempted above that ye are able; but will with the temptation also make a way to escape, that ye may be able to bear it." What this means is, God will not put more on you than you can bear when you are trusting in Him. However, if you are not trusting God, then you are bearing the weight yourself. If you're walking in the flesh, you are not going to be able to carry the load of the valley. Walking in the Spirit is going to keep you focused and empower you to trust Jesus to carry your burden.

> **Though we fail to trust God in our various valleys, He still unconditionally loves us.**

Job's wife didn't trust the Lord like her husband. She said to him, "...Dost thou still retain thine integrity? curse God, and die" (Job 2:9). We see the contrast of two people: one was letting the Lord carry the load, and the other was trying to carry it herself.

Today, what a blessing it is to see Job's life in hindsight, and to know that if Job went through his valley as he did, then there is hope that I can get through what *I* am going through, likewise! We can see that Job's situation was from God, that it had a divine purpose and outcome with the focus of a test to show forth God's glory. Just always remember what Philippians 1:6 states, "Being confident of this very thing, that he which hath begun a good work in you will perform it until the day of Jesus Christ:" Have you been guilty of being like Job's wife? Or do you have someone in your life like Job's wife, who is losing sight of God's working. Let me challenge you to be like Job and to keep your integrity and your love for the Lord.

Looking back to our relationship with the Lord/Shepherd, though we fail to trust God in our various valleys, He still unconditionally loves us. He is there for you, and like the prodigal's father, He will receive you if you will look to Him. If you stray in the valley, God understands, and since the creation of mankind, His children have done just what you're doing. However, God never created man to live independent of Him. As the Bible states in Proverbs 13:15, "Good understanding giveth favour: but the way of transgressors is hard." He will search you out as a lost sheep that has wandered from the fold. "What man of you, having an hundred sheep, if he lose one of them, doth not leave the ninety and nine in the wilderness, and go after that which is lost, until he find it" (Luke 15:4).

In the next chapter, we will see, after we are assured in our Shepherd/Sheep relationship, and we see God's purpose, plan, and outcome with a particular focus, how to watch God unfold His plan in our lives.

CHAPTER 4

PAINTING THE BIG PICTURE

I woke up one morning, and after praying, learned that all my children had been killed. Then, the next day, all of my wealth and fame was taken away. Another day came, and then my health was gone, and my wife and friends turned against me. I knew I had done no wrong to cause this in my life. But, I also knew that there was no fault to be found in my God and His watchful care of me. How could this be, that God is so great, and at the same time, my life be such a mess? I know that God will work in my life and bring about something beautiful from these tragedies.

Based on the Life of Job

> For I know that my redeemer liveth,
> and that he shall stand at the latter day upon the earth.
> Job 19:25

> To appoint unto them that mourn in Zion, to give unto them beauty for ashes, the oil of joy for mourning, the garment of praise for the spirit of heaviness...
> Isaiah 61:3

The Painting of the Picture of Our Lives

Two preachers were arguing one day about eternal security versus not having it. In their back and forth debate, one preacher finally asked, "If you were in a lifeboat, and you decided to jump out of the boat, wouldn't you die in the water?"

The other preacher said, "No, not really. Let me illustrate: My son and I were out on a river canoeing. My son was two or three years old, he was a little tyke, and we were going through some rapids, and I was scared he was going to fall out. My son started to cry a little bit, so I went up to the front of the canoe and grabbed him. I held on to him so he wouldn't fall out of the canoe."

The other preacher who was arguing against eternal security said, "That's where you're wrong. What if your kid had squirmed out of his jacket and jumped out of the canoe willingly?"

The other preacher answered, "You don't understand. I didn't have him by the coat. I had him around the waist, and I wasn't letting go."

In every situation that comes in our lives, God has us by our waist. The one preacher who did not believe in eternal security did not see the big picture. On the other hand, the other preacher saw the story from the broader perspective. When we see that God is in control of our valleys, and when the divine trials, temptations, or chastisements come our way, and our path is illuminated by the Shepherd's purpose (1 Corinthians 10:13), this will bring about the big picture of the valley, as we illustrated in the last chapter, that working through the valleys of life is like working a puzzle, and we must keep the big picture in mind while walking in the valley. The obvious question is, "How do we see and find the big picture?"

In answer to that question, we consider our walks through the valleys. We may know that God has purposes and plans, but the prolonged period of a trial is when God reveals details for us and starts to develop the big picture in our thinking. Back before the digital days of cameras, photographers needed a dark room in order to develop pictures. Likewise, in our lives, the long dark valleys of life reveal and develop the big picture for us. For example, when a good painter paints a picture, he is very skilled, and a lot of thought and planning goes into the finished product. The painter will start with a thought and a picture in his mind, and then he will proceed to put it on the canvas.

This process evolves over a course of time. As he paints, the painter begins to paint a picture of some nice scenery. Just imagine some mountains and valleys. But then all of a sudden, he decides to add people to the painting in the midst of the trees, the forest, and the greenery. Then, the artist will take some black or brown paint and make a blotch right in the middle of this colorful background. Then, let's imagine if you were to stop the painter at the blotch and not let him paint any further. A person passing by the unfinished work would look at the painting and the blotch, and say, "Man, now that painting is worthless because there is a blotch in the middle of the painting!" However, we would know that the painting was unfinished, and if you let the painter continue his work, then the blotch would start to take shape, and the artist would begin to work his mastery, and the picture would start to come together just beautiful.

Many times, our valleys are just that way. We get a blotch on the picture of what we expect or what we can see in our lives, and before the Master Painter, our Shepherd, has the time to finish His painting and the work of His wonder on the canvas of our lives, we get so focused on the blotch that we miss the big picture. The contrast to this scenario is Joseph, who was ordained to be the leader in the nation of Israel. The process of getting him to this place of leadership was all but easy to understand. There were no great installation ceremonies, or any easy paths for him, as most of us would have dictated for a man of Joseph's character.

But the opposite was true. He was persecuted by his brethren, thrown into a deep ditch, sold into slavery, and he was sent into Potiphar's house as a slave. Then, all of a sudden, Potiphar's wife tries to seduce him, and he is put in jail for a crime he did not commit.

When he came out of the valley later, and the painting was done, the result was that he went into the palace, and God used him for the deliverance of Israel, and, likewise, his own family, who were the very ones who sold him into slavery. Joseph's valley of purpose led him through many trials, temptations, and to the palace. Each part of these made the painting of his life so beautiful. Often, it is hard for us to picture the bad and the good on the same painting. If he would have stopped letting the Master painter paint in the ditch, slave yard, or the jail, this story would have turned out totally different. I believe that it is very important that we look intently at the unfolding of the big picture during our valleys because it will help in decision making in the valleys of life.

I believe that all during the valley, Joseph saw the big picture being painted. This is seen in the fact that we never hear Joseph complaining or griping about his situations. We find in Genesis 50:20 that Joseph said, "But as for you, ye thought evil against me; but God meant it unto good, to bring to pass, as it is this day, to save much people alive." John Gill writes on this verse,

> He (God) that designed good should come by it, and he brought good out of it: this shows that this action, which was sinful in itself, fell under the decree of God, or was the object of it, and that there was a concourse of providence in it; not that God was the author of sin.[8]

God used all these negative situations in Joseph's life, as well as the lives of others around him. Let us consider a contrasting picture, with a different ending to the valley. Let us suppose that Joseph had not seen the big picture that God was painting and had painted, when it came to his brethren and all his trials. If Joseph had not been walking with the Lord through the valley and seeing the Master's plan, Joseph could have said, "Man, my brethren sold me into slavery, I'm not giving them anything, just let them starve to death!" The story and the life of Joseph would not have been what God had painted in his life if Joseph had made these poor decisions. God painted a picture of His provision, protection, forgiveness, and securing of Joseph, in spite of the circumstances, to show forth why He chose Joseph. This could not have been accomplished if Joseph had not seen God's Hand in all of his difficulties.

This point is also illustrated when I look at the beautiful earth that God has given us, the beautiful blues skies, the sandy beaches, and the crystal seas. I am awestruck at the earth's beauty. However, for there to be the beautiful mountains and oceans, there must be storms,

> **To every thing there is a season, and a time to every purpose under the heaven:**
> **Ecclesiastes 3:1**

rain, clouds, winter, and blazing hot summers. When we read Ecclesiastes 3:1, "To every thing there is a season, and a time to every purpose under the heaven," we see that it takes all the things of earth and life to complete the beauty of the earth. In the same manner, it takes all the valleys and mountains in life to make this life beautiful. Take the time to read the rest of the Ecclesiastes chapter 3; it really lays out God's handiwork in all the situations of life.

Who Is the Painting For?

Every artist who paints a picture does so with an intended audience. For example, the painting may be for him/her self to decorate the home or for someone else, or maybe it is intended for a gallery. When we go back to the Twenty-third Psalm, where the Bible says, "He leads me in paths of righteousness for..." does God say, "For your cause?" No! Does He say, "For your career?" No! The Lord says, "For His name's sake!" Many times, the valleys of my life may not have as much to do with me and my life personally, but are more designed and purposed to be used in others' lives. We will deal with this more in the section "The Road Map in the Valley."

If you aren't in a valley right now, you might be in the near future. You may not understand the circumstances or all the things that are going into the curriculum of your spiritual education. Maybe you are reading this and you used to walk with God a year ago, but, for the last year, you have been in the valley and have slid away from God. You have stopped walking, or maybe you've tried to run out of the valley; thus, God is not able to show you the things He wants to show you. Maybe you have looked at the picture of your life and you do not like what you see, presently. Let me urge you to take a deep breath and take all these things in perspective.

When the valleys come, we need to pray something like this: "Lord, something has come into my life; I don't understand it or what's going on. That's okay. Lord, help me to slow down and walk *through* that valley. Lord, help me to see the light at the end of the tunnel and see Your Great Hand painting the picture in my life."

With what has already been taught, I wish that I could put these principles in a pill, so that you could take the pill when you get in a valley, and/or when you are in a situation where you are about to lose hope. Then, you would see the big picture like

Joseph did. The pharmaceutical companies sell pills, and they are making millions trying to help people deal with life with their medicines. Most times, their so-called cure wears off, and the valley is still there, and your perspective has not changed.

For those who know Christ as their Saviour, and He is their Shepherd, this is where your spirituality takes the test. This is where what you have learned, seen, and read will really take fruition in your life. The question is *Will you do it now?*

CHAPTER 5

THE CRUTCHES IN THE VALLEYS

One summer day, I went out to my husband's car to look for my favorite CD. When I opened the console, I found a letter, but I did not recognize the handwriting. After reading it, I had to come to grips with the fact that my husband was having an affair. My heart sank. I could barely hold back my anger. I confronted my husband, and he confessed, repented, and ended the relationship. However, the days and months afterward were dark and deep. My feelings of rage, insecurity, and depression did not drive me to the Lord, but drove me to over analyze my beauty. I thought to myself, if I only looked better or dressed better this would not have happened. So, I went and signed up for every clothing store credit card I could find. I literally spent tens of thousands of dollars on clothes with money we did not have, justifying the addiction to spending on my husband's affair. This went on for over a year, and afterwards, ended up costing me my marriage. If only I would have trusted in the Lord rather than money and clothes to fix my emotions.

Sincerely,
Wished I Had Trusted in the Lord

What is a crutch? In the literal sense, it's a device that is given to someone who has injured a leg or can't put weight on it for some reason. These pieces of wood or aluminum are designed to take most of the weight of our bodies, and they become our temporary legs. Spiritually speaking, as we walk through the various valleys, we will

> **The bottom line is, we will lean on something in our lives, and, unfortunately, we tend to gravitate toward sinful things.**

pick up a crutch to help us walk through the valleys of our lives; these crutches include things that we lean on other than the Lord. However, we know that we are to only lean on the Lord in the valley. He is to take the weight of the valley, as the Bible states in Matthew 11:28-30:

> Come unto me, all ye that labour and are heavy laden, and I will give you rest. Take my yoke upon you, and learn of me; for I am meek and lowly in heart: and ye shall find rest unto your souls. For my yoke is easy, and my burden is light.

However, many pick up the crutch of prescription pills, drugs, alcohol, food, a person, or bad habits for help. Any crutch other than the Lord will fail to get us through the valley, but will only be used as instruments for Satan's vices in our lives.

The Crutch of Sin

Up until now, we have looked at some important tools for walking in our valleys, such as our relationship with the Shepherd, God's purposes, outcome (the light at the end of the tunnel), and seeing the big picture. These tools should be the instruments that we lean on in our mind because they are the tools that will point our focus towards the Lord and help us to walk along the valleys in our lives. However, many times, sin and other things can become what we lean on in the valley. The bottom line is, we will lean on something in our lives, and, unfortunately, we tend to gravitate toward sinful things. Then, these crutches of sin will be very, very hard to get out of our lives.

Think about it, the teenage years are hard years with peer

pressure, hormones, and big decisions that need to be made. This is a time when we often find ourselves in valleys, and we never come out. Statisticians tell us that eighty percent of those who are saved, are saved before the age of twelve. I would add to that statistic, and say, that eighty percent of those who backslide, do so in their teenage years. General research

> **The sins that you put in your life between the ages of eight and eighteen are the sins that you will struggle with the rest of your life.**

indicates that 70% of teens who are involved in a church youth group will stop attending church within two years of their high school graduation.[9] I believe what happens is, in these teenage years, valleys come into our lives, and they will either lead us closer to Christ or away from Him.

If we get away from the Lord in a valley, then we will allow sin to creep into our lives. The sin that we allow in our teens becomes ingrained in us. I say all the time, "The sins that you put in your life between the ages of eight and eighteen are the sins that you will struggle with the rest of your life." A question to consider is, *How much of our reactions to our valleys were started when we were young?*

The reason that sin becomes our crutch in the valleys is that typically, if you're in the blessings of God on the mountaintops, it is easier to live victoriously. In the blessings, they prod you along (that finicky sheep syndrome we talked about earlier). However, what happens when you get in the valley? The *"...sin that so easily doth beset us"* (Hebrews 12:1) is what we run to rather than God, and we get some temporary satisfaction out of these sinful crutches. There is pleasure in sin for a season, and we run to it, seeking some pleasure from the valley rather than leaning on the Lord and finding satisfaction in the Lord. Satan has planted many of these stumbling blocks in the valley path. These sins or crutches are other ways to take away from God's Glory. That is why the Bible says clearly in 2 Corinthians 2:11,

> **We have a great God and Shepherd, Who has supplied us with the Spirit of God and the Word of God to guide us into all truth and every situation.**

"Lest Satan should get an advantage of us: for we are not ignorant of his devices." In your hallway of faith, there will be many temptations to stop at and trust, other than things pertaining to the Lord.

If we do not live the Christian life, or if we do not walk through the valley of the shadow of death without fear, it is not God's fault; nor is it Satan's fault. It is ours! We choose our decisions. Our Lord has given us all things that we need to help us lean and look to Him in the valleys. We have a great God and Shepherd, Who has supplied us with the Spirit of God and the Word of God to guide us into all truth and every situation. If we fail to see these facts and don't make them a reality in our lives, this lack of trust could have a dangerous proposition for us and potentially make or break us in our valleys.

Let me illustrate. We have picnic tables now in the backyard of the church, where I pastor. They are really nice picnic tables from an outlet center shopping mall in our area that was closing down. These were given to the church. I was using a church member's box truck one day, to pick up the tables. When returning the truck to his big warehouse, I was all excited about these new tables. So as I was talking to another church member who was with me, I said, "I'm going to pull the truck up in the warehouse for him." (Normally, the guy who owned the truck did this because there was very little room on the side of the box truck and door way.) I looked, and the garage door was open. As I was looking at the side mirrors, making sure I had enough room, suddenly, I heard a *Crunchhhhhh!* I pulled back and realized that the garage door was down just a few inches. I did not have enough headroom, and I ripped the door off his warehouse.

I told you that story because this is similarly what happens to us in the valleys. We get to looking too intently at the mirrors (or things), or we lean on something other than the Lord. So, as we are looking to see if the mirrors are okay, in our over concern, we forget about looking ahead or above, which is the Lord Jesus Christ, and we miss the most dangerous situation in our valley; thus, we develop a crutch in our lives. How many times do we find ourselves worrying about what we are going to do or what will be the end result? This is often the focus of the valley. Again, this is where faith comes to play. I have found that for me, when my faith is strong, I don't look back fretting or look around worrying, but I am more likely to look up to the Lord in faith.

Another illustration of how dangerous it can be veering off of God's chosen path is, when traveling down the highway, if we are distracted by something on the side of the road, and we focus on it more than the road ahead, we will eventually veer off the road. This is similar to what happens to us in the valley. Anytime we look or lean on anything or anyone in the valley other than the Lord, it will cause problems in our lives and draw us to veer in another direction. These negative crutches actually become our trust; thus, consequently, these crutches slow us down in our walk.

I am not a very fast runner, but if you put me in a race against a person on crutches, I could outrun him, easily. As much as we do not want to run in the valley, nor do we want to go too slow, we want to be walking in stride with the Lord through the valley, as illustrated in Hebrews 5:12, "For when for the time ye ought to be teachers, ye have need that one teach you again which be the first principles of the oracles of God; and are become such as have need of milk, and not of strong meat." These people had gone through a valley, which seemingly was a test of faith and doctrine, but they had reverted back to parts of their old faith of Judaism. You see, God has great timing and pace for our lives, and as we are commanded in Ephesians 5:16, "Redeeming the time, because the days are evil," as well as Hebrews 12:1, "...let us run with patience the race [or valley] that is set before us," we need to be in step and stride with the Lord and not let the crutches of this world slow us down.

Now, among all the promises in the Bible, one of the great ones is the return of the Lord Jesus. I really believe that the Lord could come back today, and I could stand before Him soon and give an account. If I am in the middle of a valley, I will be judged by how I am running when He comes back (Hebrews 12:1). That is why the Bible says to remove the sin which so easily besets us. Our crutches slow us down and become a placebo to what we really need, which is to trust in the Lord and look to Him during the valley. Let us look at some other specific crutches and how we can lean on them.

The Crutch of Death

So, as we take a refreshed look back at Psalm 23,

Psalm 23:4 – "Yea, though I walk through the valley of the shadow of death, I will fear no evil: for Thou art with me; Thy rod and Thy staff they comfort me."

I think the fear of death could be a major crutch in the life of

God's sheep. As addressed earlier, the valley in Psalm 23 is not for the purpose of death. Jesus Christ has already taken care of death for us through His Son. I know some Christians who are fearful of death, probably because they have a fear of the unknown and they are not gripped into the promise of Heaven like they should be. The Word of God says, "absent from the body...present with the Lord" (2 Corinthians 5:8). We, as Christians, look forward to Heaven. Paul said of himself in Philippians 1:23, "For I am in a strait betwixt two, having a desire to depart, and to be with Christ; which is far better:" Paul knew that God had a purpose and plan for his life, and death did not scare him, but instead, death excited him. God, likewise, has a purpose and plan for our lives also, and death should not scare us and become a crutch.

> The fear of death, many times, paralyzes us and makes us preoccupied with death more than life.

You notice what the promise says, "I will fear no evil: for Thou art with me..." The psalmist is not worried that death will come, and by the end of the Psalm, he reassures himself and us of Heaven. You are not to focus on the reality of death, unless you are not truly saved or born again. In that case, you need to take care of this right away. If you are a Christian, then the reality of your life in Christ should be of preeminence. The fear of death, many times, paralyzes us and makes us preoccupied with death more than life. So let's not let this become a crutch for us.

Death could be also looked at as a way of escape, namely, suicide. I believe that is why we see suicide so prevalent in society today. So many have left the Lord and tried to deal with life and valleys through secular means, other than Him. Suicide can become a crutch to escape the misery of the valley in which we are not trusting God. The sense of hopelessness leads to this crutch. Suicide, many times, seems like the only way out of the valley for some people.

For example, let's say that a person gets in a valley and secures a crutch, and then God starts to chastise that person, in order for the person to repent of the crutch and to get back to trusting in the Lord. What often happens is, the longer the person continues unrepentant, the more the Lord has to chastise him or her. Thus, since the chastisement has little or no effect on the person because of his or her free will, the person will continue to walk further away from the Lord. Consequently, the valley only gets deeper and heavier because he or she is fighting against the Lord, rather than walking with Him.

An illustration of this is found in the discipline of a child. Sometimes you can whoop the fire out of a child (southern term-"whoop"), and the child will just look at you afterward. The child did not receive "the board of education upon the seat of instruction." It may take a few times to get your point across. A good parent with proper discipline will continue to be more creative and use necessary action to instill the lesson in the child.

Sometimes, even as God's people, we get in the valley and we do not respond correctly. Our Great Shepherd will send as many valleys as He needs to work in our lives. "Being confident of this very thing, that he which hath begun a good work in you will perform it until the day of Jesus Christ" (Philippians 1:6). The lesson here is, do not give up, but give in and look up. Death will not come until God is ready, and death is not a way of escape.

The Crutch of Denial

There is another crutch, the crutch of denial, which can be very dangerous. Denial is when we are not willing to admit our condition and/or our situation. Today, there is a rise of the "power of positive thinking" generation, which teaches, essentially, that if you stay optimistic and not think negatively, then there will be no problems. Though I believe that the mind is powerful, the mind, however, does not have the ability to change circumstances. Only God can change our circumstances or eliminate a valley through us, as we look to Him.

Even with secular twelve step programs, many say that realizing you have a problem is the first step to recovery. Being in denial of the fact of a valley is to be in denial of the purpose and outcome of the valley, and this denial is very dangerous. Consequently, you will never come out of the valley with success.

In the Book of Jeremiah, chapter six, this very subject is addressed, in which God is warning His people to flee Judea because the Chaldeans were planning their attack.

Jeremiah 6:9-15 goes like this:

> Thus saith the LORD of hosts, They shall thoroughly glean
> the remnant of Israel as a vine: turn back thine hand as a

grape gatherer into the baskets. To whom shall I speak, and give warning, that they may hear? behold, their ear is uncircumcised, and they cannot hearken: behold, the word of the LORD is unto them a reproach; they have no delight in it. Therefore I am full of the fury of the LORD; I am weary with holding in: I will pour it out upon the children abroad, and upon the assembly of young men together: for even the husband with the wife shall be taken, the aged with him that is full of days. And their houses shall be turned unto others, with their fields and wives together: for I will stretch out my hand upon the inhabitants of the land, saith the LORD. For from the least of them even unto the greatest of them every one is given to covetousness; and from the prophet even unto the priest every one dealeth falsely. They have healed also the hurt of the daughter of my people slightly, saying, Peace, peace; when there is no peace. Were they ashamed when they had committed abomination? nay, they were not at all ashamed, neither could they blush: therefore they shall fall among them that fall: at the time that I visit them they shall be cast down, saith the LORD.

In verses 9-15, God describes what will happen to them and the reasons they would not listen and leave. The reason for their stubbornness was that they were covetous. The prophets who would not warn them held back because they were prophets for worldly gain.

These false prophets claimed prosperity in the midst of valleys. Jeremiah 6:13 says, "For from the least of them even unto the greatest of them every one is given to covetousness; and from the prophet even unto the priest every one dealeth falsely." Then God says in 6:14, "They have healed also the hurt of the daughter of my people slightly, saying, Peace, peace; when there is no peace." They said there was peace, but there was no peace, no matter how much they tried to conjure it up.

> **Many Christians fall in this same type of trap of trying to ignore that there is a real problem or valley.**

Many Christians fall in this same type of trap of trying to ignore that there is a real problem or valley. They may turn to substances and/or other addictions to get through the rough days. The addictions take their mind off their problems. These addictions could be anything from sleep, food, drugs, alcohol, prescription drugs, or anything that will distract them from the immediate circumstances. The more one avoids the valley, the worse the valley gets because it never goes away. We are only ignoring it. The great thing about being a Christian is that we don't need to be in denial in the valley, but instead, we can be marching into the trouble at hand, like a powerful army in battle.

The Crutch of Experience

Part of this particular crutch will be dealt with in more detail in the section, "Putting Everything in Perspective." It is worthy to note here in this section, that experience in one valley cannot be treated like gospel in other valleys. We have seen, concerning all the different aspects of the valleys, that there is no template or no one size fits all plan, because many valleys have different focuses.

I grew up in a very turbulent home. It was a divorced family twice over, and, needless to say, it was not a Christian environment. I learned to deal with problems in life by complaining about them, feeling sorry for myself, and seeking revenge when at all possible. It goes without saying that this is not a Christian's way of dealing with situations that come into our lives.

Over the course of time, after I became a Christian, I had to retrain my thinking about people and situations that would come against me. This did not happen overnight; but through God using the valleys in my life, I realized that I could not get through this life on my own. I needed the Lord to help me. The Lord did this through the process of changing my thinking. When I got saved, He allowed valleys to do this work in my life.

Though we get saved and have a new life in Christ, we bring baggage into the relationship with our Lord and Shepherd. Many Christians have never learned this new way of thinking. They still trust the way they learned to deal with problems as young people and adults rather than the way the Lord would have them to. Many times, they just deal with problems and valleys similar to how their parents did.

We, as Christians, cannot even bank on our past victories or past failures before salvation or after becoming a Christian to get us through the valleys. The only thing we can be rest assured of is that God is with us presently. For example, when I took my first pastorate after Bible College, I thought to myself, *This will be a great opportunity for a young pastor right out of school.* The opportunity looked like a great one, and I knew it was the will of God. I knew there would be challenges in this particular church, but I was geared up for the challenge.

I was voted in, and within a week of being at the church, we found out that the church had more problems than those in a fifth grade math book! The problems were unknown to me or to the church at large before I came. There was

> **My grace is sufficient for thee: for my strength is made perfect in weakness.**
> **2 Corinthians 12:9**

a need to build confidence in the leadership again, and we were somewhere around sixty thousand dollars behind in the bills of the church. The present offerings were not even covering seventy percent of the expenses. To sum this up, we were sunk, and we were still sinking.

After that first week, I went to my office, sat there, and started to talk to the Lord. I prayed something like this, "Lord, You knew all about these problems. The church and I had no way of knowing all these problems were here; thus, we did not create them. Lord, you called me here, and I know that for sure. However, are You sure You made the right decision in bringing me here? You see, I know some of the people that put their resumes in here to be the pastor. These men are older and have much more experience with people; they are more familiar with the finances of a church, and they have been in ministry for twenty or so years. Lord, I have no experience as a pastor. I have never worked in the administration of a church. I have never even written a church check or even had a home mortgage. The deacons and people have never dealt with situations of this magnitude before now. You know that those other pastors would have done a much better job in leading this church, and basically, Lord, I admit, I don't know what to do!"

I sat in my office pondering my prayer. Then I read the Scripture, 2 Corinthians 12:9, "And he said unto me, My grace is sufficient for thee: for my strength is made perfect in weakness. Most gladly therefore will I rather glory in my infirmities, that the power of Christ may rest upon me." The Lord spoke to me in a small still voice in my heart and said in essence, "This situation called for someone with no experience. Those other preachers had experience, but they would have relied on what they knew to do. This situation was so complex, that I needed someone who would just let Me tell him what I needed done step by step."

From that day on, my thinking changed. I didn't need man's wisdom and experience; I only needed the Lord's help. Within the next few months, God blessed and the bills were paid. Even though the church finances were in a rough shape at that time, the bank refinanced with us and even dropped our interest rate from eleven percent to seven percent, which took our monthly mortgage from $5,550.00 down to $4,500.00 per month. We caught up on all our bills, and God continued to bless. If I were to continue to tell what God has done since then, it would borderline on bragging. I know of too many churches that have closed down and split over much less than we went through in those early days, but we relied on the movement and the wisdom of God to get us through.

This victory had nothing to do with me. I only did what God told me to do, and I watched Him work. I stated that I was changed from that day on. The evidence that proves my transformation is the fact that I still pastor with this same idea, and I take steps in my life from the lessons learned in this valley. God gives us experience; thus, we are to learn from and use our experience. However, we are not to trust in experience. "Trust in the LORD with all thine heart; and lean not unto thine own understanding" (Proverbs 3:5). Experience should never become a crutch or something to lean on other than the Lord. The universal principle regarding experience is a whole hearted trust in the Lord.

My Crutches Can Become Others' Crutches

As I just stated, I truly believe in the imminent return of the Lord. I also believe that while it could happen tomorrow, it could also be a hundred years or maybe two hundred years from now. I just do not know for sure, and Jesus purposed it that way. If the Lord does not come back really soon, then that means my children will grow up and eventually have children, and they will be living in the future. Most of my actions and reactions in the valley will naturally pass on to my future generations. The Word of God teaches that sin passes to the third and fourth generation.

My decisions in the valley today and what becomes a crutch for me could affect others, likewise.

You take one guy who goes to prison and his behavior likely passes on to at least one of the children, if not all. The children, and all those who watch him, are at high risk of following his pattern. They could, thus, make the same bad decisions that he made. They follow him by example. However, there are some children who watch their "bad influence" parents and feel driven to behave the exact opposite. But unfortunately, that is not always the case.

If children grow up in a family where there is alcoholism, then the children will more than likely have the same problem with alcohol. The same is true with anger issues, divorce, and any kind of substance abuse. We know that if these children trust in the Lord, they can reverse this process. The reality is that many will not trust in the Lord, and Mom or Dad's crutches will be passed on. That is why this is so important for not only ourselves, but for the young people who are watching us, so that they see us trust in the Lord during the valleys. One of the tragedies that parents are doing to their children today is, they are teaching their children that they can get through this life without God and His church; thus resulting in only forty percent of born again Christians attending church regularly, and of those same people, there is no regular Bible reading and prayer time in the home. Our children see this and have no concept of turning and trusting in God in the valleys of life. Now, I am in no way saying or justifying that people's actions or reactions to life are their mother's and/or father's fault. However, I am stating that statistically, there is a high possibility that they will follow in a parent(s)' pattern. It is everyone's personal decision to follow the Lord during the trials and troubles of life.

One great thing about valleys and this walk with the Lord that we have was explained earlier in an illustration; in school, you cannot go to the next grade until you pass the tests, or until you understand the valley's lessons first. God does let us do makeup tests. Learning the lesson from the valley enables you to do what is right in the first valley, so that you can move on to the next valley in life. One valley victory enables us to be victorious in the next. We will cover this point later. But just like Moses on the back side of the desert, this was a preparation for his task later.

What have become your crutches? The important point about crutches is that you recognize them. I have already stated that the wonderful perk about walking through the valley as a Christian is that we have our Shepherd. He is a God of second chances. We can learn from bad decisions in the valley, recognize our lack of trust, along with all our crutches, and get back on track and start walking through the valley once again.

CHAPTER 6

THE MAP IN THE VALLEY

O, Lord, here I sit, lonely and confused. It is cold and dark here. Lord, I don't know what to do or where to go. My son has raped my daughter; my other son has killed that son. I have morally blown it, and my kingdom has been taken away and overthrown by my rebellious son. What do I do next? Where can I go? Will you restore my life again? What will be my legacy?

God's Answer: Solomon

Based on the Life of King David

Most of us, when we plan our vacations, first decide the destination, then a means to get us there. If we are driving, we get our maps, or we go on the internet and plan our route. We will decide what car to take, how much money we need for gas and a place to stay when we arrive. Likewise, as we journey through life, we need a plan. Our destination is Heaven, and our vehicle to get us there is faith. The gas that fuels the car is the Spirit of God in our hearts. The road of our lives is paved with the divine purpose and outcome, while seeing the big picture and trusting in the Lord.

We do need a plan or a map for our journey through this life. The map is the Word of God, which gives us a course of action, from which our Shepherd fully guides. This map (Truth of the Bible) is sort of like a trail through the deep woods (World). We take the path that is before us and stick to it. To get off the trail could very well mean that we get lost. This map of action is what Jesus was talking about in Matthew 7:13-14, "Enter ye in at the strait gate: for wide is the gate, and broad is the way, that leadeth to destruction, and many there be which go in thereat: Because strait is the gate, and narrow is the way, which leadeth unto life, and few there be that find it."

Turn-by-Turn Directions

With the recent invention of the new turn-by-turn satellite navigation system (GPS), you can put an address in the system; a voice tells you when to turn and when to stop at your destination. This is the way God must lead us through the various valleys of life, with its many complexities, hinging upon our decisions and others' decisions.

When we walk through the valleys, at times, the purpose can even change in the middle of the valley. So a complete map may not be what is best for us and can become obsolete in the middle of the journey because of God's rerouting in our lives. Many times this roadmap in the valley will not even be figured out by us completely until later in the valley experience. God gives us the amount of direction we need and/or can handle. There are parts of the journey that will only be revealed in God's timing for a very specific purpose.

Years ago, I went out to get into my car and discovered that my car had a flat. Needless to say, I was frustrated because I was going to be late for work. I changed the tire and started on my trip. As I was traveling down the road, I saw some flashing lights ahead. There had been an accident. The accident had happened about ten minutes before I arrived, which was the amount of time it took me to change my tire. Like so many of us who have had the opportunity to experience God's providence like this, we know that it is very possible that God had to flatten my tire in order to avoid an accident. Have there been times like this in your life also? How did the Lord reveal His turn by turn directions to you?

It is okay for me to have a plan, but God knows the path ahead.

Vance Havner says,

> I thank God for the Unseen Hand, sometimes urging me onward, sometimes holding me back; sometimes with a caress of approval, sometimes with a stroke of reproof; sometimes correcting, sometimes comforting. My times are in His hand. . . . The Unseen Hand may be obscured at times by the fogs of circumstance but just because we can't see the sun on a cloudy day doesn't mean that it isn't there.[10]

When you travel on the interstate, at every mile you see a marker with a number on it that tells you where you are on your trip. Likewise, as God leads in life, there are different stages and markers that show us that we are on the right trek. In these stages of God revealing, I look at my map, the Word and the Will of God, His Purposes, His Plans, and His Big Picture, and make sure I am still right.

What started out as a valley, allowed by the Lord for the purpose of a test, can change even in the middle of the valley, especially if we end up making some bad decisions. The valley's purpose can change, but it will still move us toward making right decisions. Once we have fulfilled the purpose of making right decisions, then we can get back focusing on the Lord and His original purpose of testing our faith. So, on the journey, as we walk with the Lord, we need to be careful to always be listening to the Voice of the Lord and His moving and working.

Watch Out Complaining
About Directions

With the purpose sensitive map through the valley, life can get a little frustrating. It seems like, just the time you get on track; you end up getting lost again. Have you ever taken a trip based on someone else's directions or directions from the internet, and no matter how good the directions were, if you got lost, it seemed to be the direction's fault? We say, "If these directions were right. . ." or "Where did they learn to give directions? I could have found this place better on my own!"

There is a level of truth that we can get bad directions from people and the internet at times; but when the directions come from the Lord, they are always very clear. Even the directions that we get from people can be much better than we give them credit for. Often, what happens is, we look at the directions briefly when we start off on the trip, and then we don't look at them again until after we are lost. We assume that we had the directions in our mind, but we really did not.

Remember the nation of Israel who questioned God (Exodus 14:11)? The nation came to Moses and said in paraphrase, "Were there no graves back in Egypt that we could have died there?" They started questioning God's man, Moses, and questioning God's character. They started questioning God's directives and provisions in their life.

God got to the point where He said (in my words), "Moses, step back. I'm getting ready to annihilate these people." Moses said to Lord, "Remember your promises, God." Then God thwarted His divine wrath upon the nation of Israel. So we better be careful not to bicker at God, as we are seeking turn by turn directions; it could get us a one way ticket to Heaven. He has given us clear directions, but we are the ones who are not listening.

> You can be assured that God will never lead you outside the boundaries of His Word.

The Word and the Spirit and the Reading of the Map

Psalms 37:23 says, "The steps of a good man are ordered by the LORD: and he delighted in his way." The road map is taking what we know (the Word of God) and directions from the Lord through the Spirit of God, and putting it to action. The map is to be read and interpreted by faith. That is why James says that faith without works is dead. Faith is looking and acting based on God's Word. Faith is not blind because God gives me His Word. Our faith is based upon His Word and on God's character. Hebrews 13:8 says, "Jesus Christ the same yesterday, and to day, and for ever."

The only tangible map we have is His Word, but it is the Spirit of God that interprets it for us. The Spirit speaks to us and tells us through the Word to turn and/or stop. We can be assured that God will never lead us outside the boundaries of His Word. By faith and the Spirit of God, we entrust our lives to the Word. Now, I am going to take for granted that you believe that the Word of God is inspired and infallible. Those who have successfully walked through the valleys of life all have one thing in common, and that is they base their lives on the Word of God.

Let us look at some selected verses from Hebrews 11. "Now faith is the substance of things hoped for, the evidence of things not seen" (Hebrews 11:1).

> **We can be assured that God will never lead us outside the boundaries of His Word.**

"Through faith we understand that the worlds were framed by the word of God, so that things which are seen were not made of things which do appear" (Hebrews 11:13). "But without faith it is impossible to please him: for he that cometh to God must believe that he is, and that he is a rewarder of them that diligently seek him" (Hebrews 11:6). Hebrews 11:13-14 says,

These all died in faith, not having received the promises, but having seen them afar off, and were persuaded of them, and embraced them, and confessed that they were strangers and pilgrims on the earth. For they that say such things declare plainly that they seek a country.

These were people who were in a valley, but at the same time, they received a promise from God (His Word) and did not falter, but finished well.

Hebrews 11:15 says, "And truly, if they had been mindful of that country from whence they came out, they might have had opportunity to have returned." The rest of the chapter describes these people's great persecution and trials for their faith in what God told them. A great quote that I heard years ago was, "God will never lead you where faith cannot keep you." God got these men through their valleys listed here in Hebrews 11, and likewise, He can do it for you also. The sheep in the fold of the shepherd were always listening for the shepherd.

Jesus uses this illustration in John 10:2-5:

> But he that entereth in by the door is the shepherd of the sheep. To him the porter openeth; and the sheep hear his voice: and he calleth his own sheep by name, and leadeth them out. And when he putteth forth his own sheep, he goeth before them, and the sheep follow him: for they know his voice. And a stranger will they not follow, but will flee from him: for they know not the voice of strangers.

Then Jesus says in John 10:27, "My sheep hear my voice, and I know them, and they follow me:" This is where we see if we really have a relationship with the Great Shepherd; we will know His voice and believe that He is directing us, and we will follow Him.

Historians say that when the shepherds came in from the fields, they would house their sheep with other shepherds' flocks. They would be together in a large arena-type stockade, and a porter would

> **My sheep hear my voice, and I know them, and they follow me. John 10:27**

guard the entrance. The shepherd would come to the porter, and he would yell for his sheep, and they would come to him. They knew his voice from hearing it so often out in the fields. Jesus says that the stranger's voice would not even register with them. The reason the sheep would know their shepherd's voice was because they were so used to hearing and obeying it in the valleys and pastures. Direction during the valley is always as close as an open Bible and the Spirit of God guiding us.

In Psalm 10:1-2, the Bible says, "Why standest thou afar off, O Lord? why hidest thou thyself in times of trouble?" Think about what David is saying: "God, where are you when all this stuff is going on?" He states that God is not there! Verse two says, "The wicked in his pride doth persecute the poor: let them be taken in the devices that they have imagined." Here, we see David focusing on the heathen rather than the Lord. Skipping on down to verses 16 – 18,

> The LORD is King for ever and ever: the heathen are perished out of his land. LORD, thou hast heard the desire of the humble: thou wilt prepare their heart, thou wilt cause thine ear to hear: To judge the fatherless and the oppressed, that the man of the earth may no more oppress.

What I want to show you here, overall, is that many of the Psalms are like this. David starts out talking to God, and He says in essence, "Why is this going on in my life?" and, "Why do the heathen rage, and the people imagine a vain thing..." (Psalm 2:1). He starts out using his own reasoning, and he is confused and distressed. But notice that by the end of the chapters, he has already answered himself. God has answered David, through His Word, regarding Who He is; David listened.

God never experiences hindsight.

We are God's sheep, and we just need to listen a little more clearly. God does not want us to blindly walk around when we are in the valley. God may not give us all the details, but with each step we take, based on His Word, God will guide us and encourage us.

People often say, "Hindsight is 20/20." With God, that is not true. God never experiences hindsight, and He is never taken off guard. As we are following the Shepherd through the valley with Him, it does not have to be all hindsight lessons learned for us either. God reveals details and actions to us when we need them, as we trust in Him.

We have this assurance, like the hymn says, "One day at a time, Sweet Jesus." Based on this principle, I will pray: "Each step I take, dear Jesus." I will ask God, "Why am I in this valley?" or, "Why am I in the trouble I am in?" or, "Why am I in the midst of these financial problems?" or, "Why am I in the midst of these marital problems?"

or, "Why am I in the midst of all that I am going through?" I will go on to say, "I know that You have allowed this and have an outcome based on Your will. I am going to look for the light at the end of the tunnel and follow the road map of Your Word."

A timely tip for sticking to the road map of God's Word (my course of action) is that I personally search out His Word and see how God has worked in other people's lives. I must look at their valleys and situations that they were in and look at how they responded. If we do this, we will find, at times, many valuable responses to situations that great men of God have made.

The Scope and Limited Map in the Valley

Now, it's time to address who the valley is for. There are times when the valley is obviously for someone else. Maybe the valley is just for Jesus' glory. Remember Lazarus? What did the sisters say? In essence, they said, "Jesus, we know that You love us. We know that we called for You. If You had only come a little bit quicker, our brother, Lazarus, would still be living." He said, "...This sickness is not unto death, but unto the glory of God..." (John 11:4).

This great truth of the valley being all about God's glory is a great driving force, enabling you and me to stop taking the valley so personally. This was Jesus' secret for walking through His valley, and the motivation was that He knew who was going to benefit from His valley (you and I). He came to die, knowing that He was going to be rejected, scorned, lied about, sold out, denied, beaten to a bloody pulp, and crucified. He came knowing what would befall Him. Like in the book of Hebrews, chapter twelve, verse two, the Bible says, exhorting us, "Looking unto Jesus the author and finisher of our faith; who for the joy that was set before him endured the cross, despising the shame, and is set down at the right hand of the throne of God." He saw the purpose, picture, outcome, and the map that ended up leading to our salvation and His glory. The old statement goes, "It was not the nails that held Him to the cross, but it was His Love for me."

One's valley could also be likened unto the Lord's valley, Whose sole purpose was for the souls of humanity. For instance, our valley could be for the benefit of someone that we do not even know. It could be for God; for His purpose of bringing glory to Himself through us. At times, the valley may even start out for us and turn into more of a benefit for someone else. Let's say, for example, that I go into a financial trial for the sole purpose of God moving in my heart to tithe. This experience could also turn into a benefit for my wife, as she sees God's provisions and learns to trust in the leadership of God in her husband's life.

The valleys can change purpose, application, and scope right in the middle of the trouble. God can only reveal to us one step at a time. He knows all the details, but He only gives them to us as we need them.

Many times, we quit on God in the valley or get discouraged because we want the whole map up front. However, God only gives us turn by turn directions as we trust in Him and serve Him. During these times, we need to ask, "God, is this valley for me, or is it for You and Your glory?" or, "Is the valley for someone else?" God will reveal these realities to us each step that we take through our valley.

An example of this is Nehemiah's valley. He saw the gates of Jerusalem burned down, and he saw the people of God defenseless. He cried out, "God, why is this happening?" God saw the need and heard Nehemiah's prayer, and He opened up the way for the city walls to be brought up once again.

Nehemiah went in and suffered much persecution by Sanballat and all those wicked men who were trying to destroy the work of God. Nehemiah took his valley one step at a time, but he knew that it was in the plan and the procedure of God for him to look for God's great guidance each step of the way. Notice though, if you read the book of Nehemiah, when Nehemiah prayed, he confessed his sin, and likewise, he confessed the nation of Israel's sin. In reality, part of this valley that he and the nation of Israel were going through was to purge the nation of Israel as well as himself of sin. Once repentance was accomplished, they went to the city, then they were able to lay the foundation to the walls, then they were stacking bricks. Thus, the scope of the valleys was two-fold.

God did not give Nehemiah the whole map; He uncovered each part as Nehemiah needed it with the revealed scope. Very well, if Nehemiah would have had the whole map laid out with Sandballat and his cronies, this could have discouraged him. Do not miss the fact that Ezra had a great part in the total rebuilding of Jerusalem. Nehemiah built the wall and Ezra built the people. Prior to setting out, Nehemiah had no knowledge of Ezra as far as we know. The way through the valley was not so easy. They would have to trust in God, to hold a sword with one hand and to hold a trowel in the other hand, so they would learn to depend on God. Now, looking back and seeing how God used this great valley in the nation, as well as many others' lives, is very fascinating and encouraging, seeing that we don't know all the facts up front, but God does.

Remember earlier, I told you about my mother dying during the writing of this book? When I went back to my hometown in Virginia, the Lord opened up doors that I could not have imagined. For both the wake and the funeral, the Lord gave me the opportunity to stand at the head of the casket of my mother and pass out tracts and share the Gospel of Jesus Christ to

> **God was more concerned about building their lives first, than just getting them to the Promised Land.**

hundreds of people. I had family members, whom I had never had the opportunity to share the Gospel with, coming up to me, and asking me how they could be assured they could go to Heaven. After the fact, I saw some family get saved as a result. Now, I did not have the whole map when it all started, but the final destination was to the glory of the Lord.

As stated earlier about the nation of Israel, as they wandered around, they were just a short hike from going to the Promised Land, but God led them around in circles. You may ask, "Why didn't God just kill them or lead them to the Promised Land?" God was more concerned about building their lives first, than just getting them to the Promised Land. He did kill many of them eventually because they refused to keep going on through the valley. Only those under the age of eighteen were able to stay in the wilderness and eventually go to the Promised Land.

The valley for the nation of Israel started from the time they became slaves in Egypt, up until they reached the Promised Land. It was the nation of Israel who decided to walk in circles, rather than walking with the Lord through the valley. God led them around in circles because He had to prove them. In the valley, was the place where God, the Shepherd, proved those who were eighteen and under, to go and be reinforcements for Joshua. Joshua and his army went into the Promised Land. A fulfillment of years and years of prophecy from Abraham up were fulfilled.

We see the result now, how the Great Shepherd used one

valley in thousands of peoples' lives. Joshua and Moses probably did not understand all that was taking place as they were walking through their valleys. They were faithful to each direction that God gave them.

Imagine Moses' life. If God would have revealed to Moses all that was going to happen in the wilderness, do you think this might have discouraged Moses? God had a hard enough time getting Moses to speak. If God would have revealed all the events from the burning bush, to having to deal with Pharaoh, to God even hardening Pharaoh's heart to show His glory, to the Red Sea, to the people complaining to Moses, to having to deal with the situation of the golden calf, strange fire, and the faithless spies, what do you really think Moses' response would have been? You want to talk about a long valley?

God was ultimately faithful. During Moses' valley, God rained down manna from Heaven and gave them water out of the rock. Unfortunately, near the end, Moses smites the rock and loses his testimony in front of God's people. For this reason, Moses was not able to go into the Promised Land.

You see, part of the process that Moses was going through was to show God's power and His glory through Moses. Moses' bad decision in the valley cost him the Promised Land, but he went to Heaven. It is hard for us, when a valley comes, to stomach it many times. So, that is why we need to pray, "Dear God, why is this happening? Why am I going through this in my life?" We must be patient and not lose our faith, before God reveals the steps in the path for us.

I remember the first thing I said when I surrendered to go into ministry. "Lord, I will do anything but pastor a church." Anyone who has been a Christian for a while will know that the statement I made is very dangerous. I said to myself, "I was too young," and like Moses, I had my list of excuses. Through a series of events, I said, "I'll be a missionary." I went online looking for a Bible college that had a good missions program. There was another school that everyone from my church wanted me to go to, but I could not get peace about it. I was surfing the internet for "Missionaries" and "Baptist," and then I found a mission minded college. I looked at their missions program, put in my application, got accepted and enrolled.

I got there, and it was probably one of the darkest valleys

that I have had during my spiritual walk. I went to a college that I thought was conservative in their methods of ministry. I found out quickly that it was not. Another problem I had was that I had high expectations for those who were Bible College Christians. I thought these young believers would be the spiritually elite. I imagined having Bible studies, praying, singing "Kum By Ya," and talking about Jesus all day. It was a totally different atmosphere than I expected. (Just for the record, this was my problem and not the college's or the students'.) Then, about ten days into the college year, I called my preacher, Pastor Dewey Weaver, and I said, "This is not what I expected."

> He asked me, "How long do you think you can make it?"

> I said, "I could make it a year, I guess."

> He said, "Give it a year and then make your decision, whether to stay or go."

From the day that I called my preacher, I did not make a decision whether I was going to stay or go to another college until the last day of that school year. I gave the college my fullest ability; I gave it a real Boy Scout's try, as one would say. I even changed my thinking and expectations in some areas. At the end of the year, I made my decision that I was not returning to that school, not because I was miserable, but I made the decision by faith and what God wanted for me.

During that whole year at college, I did not understand what God had done for me. Looking back, I see two blessed reasons why God had me attend that college. The college I went to next didn't have as good of an English program. I needed English because God knew I was going to be a pastor some day. You see, if I was going to be a missionary, I did not need English as much as I would, compared to being in America, as a pastor, not counting that God knew one day that I would write this book. The second thing that God did for me that year was make me more conservative in methodology. After seeing the opposite spectrum of a more contemporized Christianity, it enabled me to really get into the Word and develop my convictions for myself, instead of developing convictions from philosophies and rules of a college. During that year, God used me in many of my friends' lives, and not counting all the people that I led to the Lord that year.

I remember a man that I worked with at a steel mill. He was a security guard and I was a janitor. He had gone to the Bible College I had gone to, but he was unsaved. From the very beginning, he was very hostile toward me because of my faith, so I just made it my mission to love him. He had become Catholic, and he would come up and debate with me about faith verses works salvation. I never would debate with him. I would talk about my freedom in Christ and how to really be saved. He was always so mad that I would not argue with him. I ended up switching jobs.

When I gave my notice, he came running to me an hour later. I thought to myself, *I guess he will try to get one last debate in before I go.* To my surprise, he approached me, and with tears welled up in his eyes, he said, "I want to let you know that I am going to miss you, and I want to let you know that you have impacted my life by not arguing with me. All those times I wanted to argue with you, you stuck to the Truth, and I am probably going to go back to a right doctrine church and really get saved."

At the end of the school year, the day before I left, one of my friends came up and handed me a popular Baptist magazine that had an article about a college in Virginia. My friend said, "Well! There is a Bible College over on the East Coast where you're from. Have you looked into it?"

From that article and the advice from my friend, I went over and visited the school and enrolled. During my education, I went to Landmark Baptist Church, in Richmond, Virginia, and there is where I met my wife, Heidi.

Dr. Jack Baskin, who I met through the college, was at Victory Baptist Church in Pleasant Prairie, Wisconsin, the year I was graduating. There, he gave Brother John Faulkner, one of the deacons, my resume. (I did not know Dr. Baskin had my resume. He got it from the Bible College without my knowledge.) Very shortly afterwards, I became the pastor of Victory Baptist Church.

Now see, what would have happened if I had quit in the valley? God wanted to use me along the way. If I would have not followed God's turn by turn directions and not let God lead me step by step and teach me, I do not believe I would be here today. Now, I firmly believe in the providence of God, but I also believe in the free will of man. I could have chosen to say, "You know what? I don't want to be here anymore! These Christians with their stinking attitudes, with their lukewarm lifestyles, I need to be where people really want to serve God!" The problem with this kind of thinking was that God had me right where He wanted me.

Think what I would have missed in my life. That is why it is so important that we walk through the valley. During the valley, I remember asking God, "Why am I here?" As I was walking through the valley that year, God was showing me these things that I just shared with you. He was encouraging me to stay in there and not quit. I became very, very happy as God was using me in the lives of others, as well as my own. Now, I say that because we also need to ask God what to do in our valleys in the future. It is not about how we want to react, or how I feel about things, but it is all about what God wants me to do. Have there been times when you wanted to quit? Do you want to quit right now? Please don't! I know that you will regret it in the long run.

Another example of this is Gideon, in Judges 6. God had told him (in my words), "I want you to go fight the battle." Gideon did not want to go, but God, through a series of events, guided him (speaking of the fleece), and God convinced him to go forth by faith. Then, as he stepped out by faith, God said, "Now, you have a great army together, but you have too many men to fight the war." God then narrowed down his army to those whose hearts were in the battle, and the rest were told to go home.

I would have been questioning God with statements such as, "That ratty-tag army is going in there to fight that great army?" and, "What are you thinking God?" God, however, showed Himself faithful. They went into battle with just a few swords, the sound of the trumpet and breaking glass, and God gave Gideon and his army just what they needed. That is why Jesus said, in Luke 12:11, "And when they bring you unto the synagogues, and unto magistrates, and powers, take ye no thought how or what thing ye shall answer, or what ye shall say"

We may be in this kind of valley in the future for our faith, and I do not know about you, but if someone says to me, "Jerry, you're going to go to jail for preaching the Gospel!" I will be scared, no doubt! However, I will believe God's faithfulness to give me the words to say in that valley. I will just wait for minute by minute directions, and for God to reveal His road map and the scope of the valley to me. That is where faith becomes real. That is where faith really comes into action in our life. We base it on our map, the Word of God, and the Spirit of God, and the providential leading of the Shepherd.

We have to remember some things. Walk, don't run. We have to keep moving, but at the same time, we must wait for God because we know each valley has a divine approval and purpose. God also has a divine outcome. During this time, it is not wrong to ask God why, for the purpose of knowing what action that He wants me to take, all for a divine outcome to come forth, with this sealed through the Word of God and the Spirit of God (roadmap). We are hopeless without these truths; we cannot make responsible decisions without them.

Let us put a little perspective on our futile abilities to guide and map out our own lives. Let me ask you a question. How much information do you and I possess? Think about all the knowledge that people had in the past. Think about all the encyclopedias. Remember that guy on "Jeopardy," Ken Jennings, who had such a long winning streak? He was very knowledgeable. Let us say, at best, that he has 0.5 percent of the knowledge that has ever been. I really think that is stretching it greatly. Now 0.5 percent is not even a percentage point. Think of that in contrast of God's knowledge of past events. He knows 100% of information in the past, and God knows everything that is happening right now. No mortal person could even claim a fraction of a percentage point in any of these categories. Likewise, our Shepherd knows everything that will happen in the future.

Compare our knowledge of the past, present, and future, contrasted to God's knowledge. The gap is staggering. There is no way we can even make intelligent decisions without God's leading. This is why I can put my faith in the Lord Jesus Christ.

We do not even register on the scale of knowledge compared to God. How many times do we find ourselves telling God what we need to do, or instructing Him on what He needs to do in the valley? There is nothing wrong with praying, but prayer, however, is not telling God what to do; it is asking the Lord to give us instructions. God has got everything under control. I have found out that what is over my head is under the feet of God. We just need to get with God's plan.

The Word of God says, "Can two walk together except they be

agreed" (Amos 3:3)? What happens is, we get out of stride and step with God, and, ultimately, our life becomes a ruin. As 2 Corinthians 5:7 says, "For we walk by faith, not by sight." We step out by every command of the Word of God and the will of God for our lives. When we do this, He will not lead us astray.

Our Individual Map

Now it is worthy to note, as we think about a road map through the valley, that there may be one destination for all, which is walking in the will of God and pleasing the Saviour; however, the way God leads us may be a little different. Often, people will say, "It seems like I am always having trials, but look at so and so, they have it made." Well, that may be true at the present time in their lives, but you do not know what it took to get them to that point. You do not know the valleys that they have had to walk through to get to the point of this so called great life. The Bible says clearly in Job 5:7, "Yet man is born unto trouble, as the sparks fly upward." That includes everyone.

The reality of our judgment of the situation would teach us that we have been too busy looking at only the good that we can see in these people, rather than all the dark days that they had to endure. The reason we do this, is that we are trying to justify our bad attitude about our valleys by using these people as an excuse.

2 Corinthians 10:12 says, "For we dare not make ourselves of the number, or compare ourselves with some that commend themselves: but they measuring themselves by themselves, and comparing themselves among themselves, are not wise." God allows valleys and situations in the lives of His children for specific purposes, unique to the individual. I cannot compare my life to anyone else's.

Likewise, there may be a different amount of trials because of bad decisions made. So, consequently, these experiences are because of the law of reaping and sowing. Valleys are very personalized. We also have special trials because of our special purpose or calling for our lives. An example of this is that the experiences that King David had were not the same as the ones that Samuel would have had. David had to fight a bear because God knew that Goliath would be ahead in the life of David. Samuel would never have to fight a bear, so he did not need to fight a bear to prepare himself.

The Bible says in Psalms 139:14, "I will praise thee; for I am fearfully and wonderfully made: marvellous are thy works; and that my soul knoweth right well." Just like my DNA and finger prints are specific to me, so is God's special purpose for me and the actions He wants me to take. I cannot look at anyone else's valleys and life and find complete direction.

The Angel's Help

Along the path of our journey through the valley, there are a host of unseen things working in the background. As the Spirit of God is working in our hearts, Satan manifests himself in circumstances and situations, placing potholes in our path.

There are, likewise, angels from the Lord in our valley helping us along the way. The Bible says in Hebrews 13:2, "Be not forgetful to entertain strangers: for thereby some have entertained angels unawares." Sometimes the angels are seen, like with Jacob and Lot in Sodom. However, most of the time, the angels are working in the background, unseen to the eye, but known in the heart and in the circumstances. Notice that Hebrews says, "Be not forgetful to entertain strangers," which I believe is indicative, that we can forget to allow the angels to work in our lives.

A story was relayed to me of the life of John Paton, who was a missionary in the New Hebrides Islands. One night, hostile natives surrounded the mission station, intent on burning out the Patons and killing them. Paton and his wife prayed during that terror-filled night that God would deliver them. When daylight came, they were amazed to see their attackers leave. A year later, the chief of the tribe converted to Christ. Remembering what had happened, Paton asked the chief what had kept him from burning down the house and killing them. The chief replied in surprise, "Who were all those men with you there?" Paton knew that no men were present; but the chief said that he was afraid to attack because he had seen hundreds of big men in shining garments with drawn swords circling the mission station. God will reveal to us and guide us correctly, and He will even send His angels to help us on the way if we will allow Him.

CHAPTER 7

PREPARATION FOR THE JOURNEY

So let us review some key points:

- We must allow the Lord to lead us and allow Him to be our Shepherd.
- Every valley has divine approval and a divine outcome—the Light at the End of the Tunnel/The Big Picture.
- We have a tendency to get crutches in the valley to lean on, rather than leaning on the Lord.
- We need a road map from the Lord that is special for God's purpose for my life or for others.
- We get directions by asking why, and we receive step by step marching orders which reveal His steps to us.

Various Valleys

When I went to Bible College, my purpose was to prepare for ministry. Like many people who go into any professional career, they go to college, university, and/or trade school to learn a profession.

I picked a school that could best prepare me for the tasks ahead. However, no Bible College can completely prepare you fully for ministry. A joke in and among preachers is, "They did not teach us this in Bible College." In ministry, as in life, situations come up that we have no preparation for.

If we were fully prepared, we would be relying on our preparation rather than the Shepherd. With all that being said, I may not be able to fully prepare you for your valleys, but I can give you some tools for your spiritual toolbox to help you work through those that come up.

For example, you may go to the doctor complaining of a spot on your skin, and within a few days, you learn that you have a fast spreading cancer and you are terminally ill. You may lose your loved one today. Listed below is a diagram of the different valleys that we can/may face. Though this list is not exhaustive, I have broken up the different areas of life in which the valleys affect us. Notice the three columns; these are based on the fact that we are Body, Soul, and Spirit, as stated in 1 Thessalonians 5:23. The valleys of life affect and afflict all these areas.

Valleys of Life

Valleys of the Heart	Valleys of the Mind	Valleys of the Flesh
Relationships	Loneliness	Injustice
Death of a Loved One	Guilt	Persecution
Betrayal	Rejection	Abandonment
Sickness of a Loved One	Failure	Abuse
Divorce	Insecurity	Addiction
Parent/Child Conflict	Growing Old	Tragedy
Incest	Dreams Shattered	Work Stress
	Loss of Faith	Financial Problems
	Spiritual Warfare	

The valleys of the mind are different than the valleys of the heart. These valleys are basically inward emotions and feelings that affect us outwardly. Whereas, the valleys of the flesh are outward based and affect the interior. All are valleys; but they are different in scope and sequence. If you will think about your valley presently, or what you have been through, and how you are affected, you will find it fits in these three categories.

The grand question is, *How can we prepare for the various valleys that come into our lives?* If your valleys are of the heart, mind, or body, would you not prepare differently for each one? I don't think so because if you take care of the inward, (mind/heart), it will also help with the exterior body valleys, such as a relationship valley or the death of a loved one.

The truths that we have learned will give us inner strength and outward protection from failure in the valley. The inner strength will be the main fortitude against all these particular areas. The particular valley is not as important as the inner strength that we have in the Lord.

Being What We Are Supposed To Be

One way to prepare for the valleys in life is to be what you already are supposed to be in the Lord on an everyday basis. The longer and more faithful a sheep is with its shepherd, the more trust and confidence it has in the Shepherd. When we, as Christians, are faithful to God during a series of tests and trials, and even, at times, during our mistakes, God will use them, and He will work in our lives to build and mold us to that place where we can handle various valleys. The process is like building muscle. You build muscle and strength by working and ripping a muscle, and then it will heal back stronger than it was before, and that is how you can lift more weights, and, consequently, get stronger. Likewise, that is what valleys do for us. The old saying is, "We develop thick skin." We develop strong, thick spiritual skin in our lives, from what drives us from our hearts. This develops from the inside out.

When we walk through the small valleys of life, then, when the big valleys come, we are much more prepared for them. As we go through these smaller valleys, and as we serve the Lord, staying faithful to the Lord, applying what we have already learned, asking, "What do You want me to do?" and "How do You want me to do it?"

each of these questions that we answer, during every valley that we go through, we will come through stronger down the road of life.

Another way to prepare is just being a basic Christian. The basic principles are all we need: praying, reading your Bible, being faithful to church, and walking in the Spirit. The Christian life is not as complicated as we make it out to be. Much of all the thousands of self-help books that are written about life are merely putting a new spin on a simple truth of the Word. The Bible simply states in Romans 8:1, "There is therefore now no condemnation to them which are in Christ Jesus, who walk not after the flesh, but after the Spirit." As Christians, all we need to do is walk in the Spirit, which will not speak of Himself, but will lead you to the Lord. "Howbeit when he, the Spirit of truth, is come, he will guide you into all truth: for he shall not speak of himself; but whatsoever he shall hear, that shall he speak: and he will shew you things to come" (John 6:13). The Spirit, spoken of here, is guided by the Word of Truth.

Likewise, as Christians, we are to devour the Word of God. That is why daily devotions are so important. If you do not do daily devotions, you will not walk with the Lord, or at least not for long. Remember, the Word is our roadmap. If you do not have a time when you pray, you are not walking with God.

How many times have I read the Word of God, and just that day, needed what I read. A great way to store up the Word in your heart is found in Rhonda Kelly's book on *Divine Discipline.* She quotes the Navigators way of getting the Word of God in our hearts. The list goes as follows: "Hear the Word, Read the Word, Study the Word, Memorize the Word, and Meditate on the Word."[11] A devotional book can be very helpful at times, or even a Bible reading schedule.

If you do not experience God's Word leading and teaching, then you are missing out. God has a message for you. It could be in your Bible reading, a sermon you've heard, or even in a good Bible centered book; but are we even listening? Could you imagine if a sheep was deaf but trying to listen to the voice of the Shepherd? "My sheep hear my voice, and I know them, and they follow me" (John 10:27). Let us never approach a valley, not hearing the Shepherd's voice.

If we know we have a tendency to struggle with sin or bad attitudes in the valley, we probably know what sins we need to be watchful of and to take heed of. Another way that I have prepared for these valleys and situations in life is to get verses out of the Bible to store up in my heart for when temptations come. I quote those verses to myself during the temptation, trial, and/or valley. Here is a sample table that can be a guide for this process. If you are struggling with your reaction in the valleys, find the verses that will help you and put them on index cards and memorize them.

SIN/TEMPTATION	THE SCRIPTURE
Anger About the Valley	Proverbs 3:5-6 Trust in the LORD with all thine heart... Jeremiah32:17,26, Psalm 23-27
Laziness in the Valley	2 Timothy 2:15 Study to shew thyself approved unto God, a workman that needeth not to be ashamed, rightly dividing the word of truth.
Self-Centeredness While in the Valley	Luke 9:23 And he said to them all, If any man will come after me, let him deny himself, and take up his cross daily, and follow me.
Self-Control in the Valley	Proverbs 25:28 He that hath no rule over his own spirit is like a city that is broken down, and without walls.
Lack of Waiting on the Lord	Isaiah 41:10 Fear thou not; for I am with thee: be not dismayed; for I am thy God: I will strengthen thee; yea, I will help thee; yea, I will uphold thee with the right hand of my righteousness.
Lack of Trust	Psalms 91:2 I will say of the LORD, He is my refuge and my fortress: my God; in him will I trust.

The use of the Scriptures in the valley is the greatest weapon against sin and discouragement in the valley. I learned a long time ago to remember that when Christians sin, it is because we fell for a lie from Satan that it is *okay* to sin. So I combat the false lies of Satan with the Truth from God's Word. Sometimes, I even sing a scriptural song to deal with the temptation at hand, which is usually based on the Scriptural Truth.

You can refer back to both tables or get a Bible Promise Book and memorize the verses that deal with the area that you are struggling with. Making sure that the sin has been dealt with in your life is important because sin is very detrimental to your walk through the valley. Psalms 66:18 says, "If I regard iniquity in my heart, the Lord will not hear me:"

If we are living in open sin, it would be hard, if not impossible, to be guided correctly through the valley. Our sin will become a stumbling block.

Hebrews 12:1 says, "Wherefore seeing we also are compassed about with so great a cloud of witnesses, let us lay aside every weight, and the sin which doth so easily beset us, and let us run with patience the race that is set before us."

Prayer

No preparation would be complete without prayer. God speaks to us through His Word. Prayer is us speaking to the Lord and Shepherd. Prayer will keep the dialogue going between us and the Lord, and it will keep us looking to Him in the dark valleys. A good rule of thumb in the valley is not to talk to anyone until we have talked to the Lord first. Amazingly, our complaining is much less when we pray first. You see, prayer not only moves God, but it also moves me. It makes me vocalize my burdens. God is speaking to my heart through His Word and the valley that He has allowed.

It is not my intent to expound on the how's and when's to pray in this book. There have been hundreds of books written about prayer by good men, one of my favorites is E.M. Bounds. Any of his books on prayer would be a great resource for you in the valley. But the point that I want to get across is that a person must pray to be prepared for the valley, as well as when we are in the valley, making sure we are looking to the Shepherd in the valley.

The Local Church

Being faithful to your local church's preaching services is a must. God prepares the man of God to speak to the hearts of His children. Being a pastor myself, many times, I will preach a message and look out to see a few empty seats. I have had the opportunity to see the people, who should have been in those empty seats, sit in my office a couple of weeks after the message was preached. By now, they have made some bad decisions in their lives. If they would have only been in church, they would have had the opportunity to hear a message that could have prevented them the pain of their bad decisions.

Another good reason to be in church is the support of other Christians. This, likewise, is a means to prepare for the upcoming valleys. I, personally, have never met anyone who could walk through the valleys consistently without the support of other Christians. "Not forsaking the assembling of ourselves together, as the manner of some is; but exhorting one another: and so much the more, as ye see the day approaching" (Hebrews 10:25). We need each other, and God knew it. Knowing that we are in the last days, and that the times are only getting worse and worse, we need each other more and more. I have often told my congregation, "You may not need me each week, but I need you."

> **I have never met anyone who could walk through the valleys consistently without the support of other Christians.**

You need the Lord, but you also need people to walk with you and to encourage you. Of course, you don't need people as much as you need the Lord, but God does use people to be a blessing to you. "And if one prevail against him, two shall withstand him; and a threefold cord is not quickly broken" (Ecclesiastes 4:12).

Godly Counsel

Adding to these truths, of just being who we are meant to be, and being in the Bible, and having fellowship with other Christians, is the fact that during the valleys, we can and should seek godly counsel. "Without counsel purposes are disappointed: but in the multitude of counselors they are established" (Proverbs 15:22). The

Bible also states that, "For by wise counsel thou shalt make thy war: and in multitude of counselors there is safety" (Proverbs 24:6). God will plant people to help you along your journey through the valley. The greatest example of this was Jonathan and David in 1 Samuel 18:1, "And it came to pass, when he had made an end of speaking unto Saul, that the soul of Jonathan was knit with the soul of David, and Jonathan loved him as his own soul." Jonathan ended up being a great asset to David when he walked through the valley. God also put Nathan in David's life when he got off track in the valley of life. It was Nathan that came to David in 2 Samuel 12, and he said to David, "Thou art the man!"

Many examples could be given, but the moral to the story is this: we need to fill our lives with people that know the Truth and principles of walking through the valleys of life. We need friends that have the fortitude to look at our actions and advise us according to the Word of God. These counselors look from outside the valleys and remind us of our responsibility to the Lord.

Here is a word of warning about secular counselors and/or psychologists. These types of people are not typically guided like you and I. Unlike Christian counselors, they are not trained according to a Biblical world view. I surround myself with a good biblical support staff. Your support system might include Christian friends, a Bible study group, or a mentor.

Doing What We Were Doing Before the Valley

When the valleys come, it might be tempting to step away from activities and service. Instead, we will benefit from sticking with these things. The best way to prepare is to basically put our life in auto pilot for the Lord. Things like reading our Bible, prayer, and Godly counsel are the things that will keep our minds stayed on the Lord in the valley. When we get in the valley and we do not know what to do, let us just continue in the things in which we know.

A perfect example of this is Hosea, a man of great valleys who had just lost his wife, and the very next day he was back out preaching. When Hosea was in the thick of that valley, he just went back out and did what he knew to do, and that was to preach. As I mentioned earlier, my mother passed away during the writing of this book. I actually preached my mother's funeral, and everyone asked me how in the world could I do that? I said that preaching is what I do at funerals; if you put me in a pew, I would be out of place. I feel more comfortable in the pulpit.

Many times, life changes so quickly, and valleys pop up so fast, that we do not have much time to think. So as we are walking with the Lord faithfully, before this earth shattering valley comes, I just continue to do the same things I was doing before the valley, namely walking and serving the Lord. This plan is always a safe bet.

Watch out for Satan

When preparing for the journeys through the valley, we need to be very careful to watch for Satan. The Bible states in 1 Peter 5:8, "Be sober, be vigilant; because your adversary the devil, as a roaring lion, walketh about, seeking whom he may devour:" Knowing that God allows Satan to tempt us and even test our faith at times, and that Satan is always looking to take us off guard, one of the ways that we can prepare for and avoid the Devil's future snares is to remember how he tripped us up in the past. In 2 Corinthians 2:11, the Bible states, "Lest Satan should get an advantage of us: for we are not ignorant of his devices."

We will find that Satan isn't very creative. He plays the same games over and over again, and he does not have any original material up his sleeves. He uses our past failures and quirks against us to get us to stumble and fall in the valley. However, I believe that we give Satan too much credit, and likewise, he becomes our escape goat for bad actions and decisions. Satan can only work in our lives in areas that we allow him. As Christians, we allow Satan a place to work in our lives, but he has no right to do so.

I firmly believe that a true Christian cannot be demon possessed, but they can be oppressed. This means we give him a place in our minds, in which he can afflict us. I must make sure that I do not surrender anything to him. When we look at Jesus' valley of temptation in the wilderness (Luke 4), we see that it was God who led Him to the wilderness. "And Jesus being full of the Holy Ghost returned from Jordan, and was led by the Spirit into the wilderness" (Luke 4:1).

Jesus was there for forty days and nights. After He had gone forty days without food, Satan came to Him, and tempted Him with food. Satan observed that Jesus had not eaten, so he tempted Him with bread. Jesus responded in Luke 4:4, "...It is written, That man shall not live by bread alone, but by every word of God." Notice here, the turn by turn directions, guided by the Word of God. Interestingly, in Luke 4:6, Satan offers power to Jesus. Like Jesus really needed it! Nevertheless, Satan could not deliver his promise to Jesus. Satan knew Jesus was tired and wearied from hunger in the wilderness. So Satan offers Jesus power. Satan is the father of lies, and he will always give you an alternative route in the valley. Remember Matthew 7:13-14, "Enter ye in at the strait gate: for wide is the gate, and broad is the way, that leadeth to destruction..." Satan's last trick was to tempt Jesus to question God's protection of Him. "For it is written, He shall give his angels charge over thee, to keep thee" (Luke 4:10). But Jesus knew His protection was only found in the Lord.

So, I prepare by looking and seeing the other valleys and how Satan has affected and afflicted me, and at the same time, being aware that he will try those tricks again. In the next section, we will talk about keeping all the things we have learned in perspective. This will tie together the points and give some application to the things we have learned.

CHAPTER 8

KEEPING IT ALL IN PERSPECTIVE

The title of this chapter really sums up much of what we have seen throughout the book about the secret to living and getting through hard times. Perspective is as simple as seeing and living all the things that we discussed. Perspective is the way you view the circumstances in life, including in the valleys. The tough part of the job though, is keeping that perspective fresh in our minds and lives during the valley.

Allow me to share this fictional story that I have written, that illustrates what our perspective needs to be.

There once was a lady who lived in a small town in the late 1800's. This lady was a widow and very poor because her husband had been killed in the Spanish American War. She was left to raise 3 boys and 2 girls on her own. However, she was a very godly lady, as were most of the people in this church centered town. Many of the town volunteered to help others, served the Lord in the church, shared their faith, and raised their children in godliness.

During the turn of the century, an economic boom happened in this small town. As mills and other factories moved in and the people prospered, the town started to change. Church meetings were replaced with social activities, and Sunday school was replaced with sports for the children.

The widowed lady, however, did not follow the tide of the town, but remained faithful to the Lord. The church that once was overflowing, now only held a few older folks and the widow's children. Many people who were now rich and had no time for God would look on her living conditions and mock her, believing that she must be under the judgment of God because she was not prospering like all the rest of them. The widow lady, however, never stopped giving praise to her Lord, and she continued to be thankful for all the provisions from Him.

The people in the town went on with their lives, living in luxury, but denying God in their lives. They provided the best clothes, education, and opportunities for their children. The people of the town used this lady and her family as an example of just how well they had it compared to her, saying things like, "At least *our* children have the newest toys" and, "Thank goodness *our* children don't have to go to that school" or, "Life is so good to *us*, look at the nice things that *we* have, unlike that widow and her children."

This went on for years, and all the children became grown. The hearts of the town's people, however, were broken. By this time, the streets were filled with saloons and brothels. Their children had grown, and many of them were either in jail, dead, or their homes were wrecked by divorce.

The widow lady, who strived under harsh and dark times of ridicule of the people, raised her children in the nurture and admonition of the Lord. Her children grew up, and her two daughters married preachers. They were used greatly by the Lord. Of the three boys, one became a doctor who cared for the sick of the town, including those who became ill due to their sinful lifestyles. The other became a missionary in Ghana, West Africa, and the third son became the preacher of one of the largest churches in the state.

Now, look at the people of the town who had the wrong perspectives. They were looking at the temporal things and opportunities and glorying in the suffering of this widowed saint. They did this to justify their lack of serving and faithfulness to the Lord. Their perspective was on the earthly, while the widow's were on the eternal. Who do you think was regretful of their perspective?

This story illustrates my point clearly. Many people around

you in the valleys will look at your situation, and judge. They will advise you and seek to determine your perspective for you in the valley. But what it boils down to is that you must have a proper view of God, and His promises must dictate your view of the valley. Look what God did for this lady.

The Old Man Verses the New Man and Our Perspective

The widow in our story had the right perspective. She focused on just what God had revealed and provided for her. She was content, and focused on the eternal, and not so much on her present condition, or of the others' so called prosperities in town. The widow lady and her family pictures the way our new perspective should be in the Lord. Just knowing that God has allowed all situations in my life, and no matter what I am going through, I am going to trust and look to the Lord.

The people in the town represent a worldly mentality and the old nature that we have before we are saved, when we focused on the earthly and a pleasured based life. This fleshly perspective can affect our walk through our valleys. This worldly perspective can be formulated way before the valley ever comes, even as far back as our childhood, especially if we are not following the Lord and His laws.

I said earlier, that eighty percent of those who are saved are saved before twelve years of age, and as well, eighty percent of our personalities are formed before we are eight years old. I will go on record and say that ninety percent of our actions and reactions, our perspective to problems, and how we deal with life are formed from eight to eighteen years of age. That is why the statement

> **We all come into the Christian life with baggage from our childhood.**

is true that the sins we put in our lives between the ages of eight and eighteen are the sins we will struggle with the rest of our lives. Going back during these impressionable years, we formulate how we act and react in valleys and problems of life. Now, at any given time that we trust in the Lord and say "yes" to the new man in Christ, though we may struggle at times, we will not be afflicted by our past.

This is why it is so important that we, as parents, walk through the valleys knowing that our children will be watching us. Likewise, more than likely, they will pattern their lives after ours. As a pastor, observing and praying for many families, I've come to see that the young children are mirrors to their families and homes. They have not been acclimated to the covering up of the real person that we do not want people to see (our hypocrisy). Many times, we can see the parents in the children, in the way they talk, act, and react to situations.

With that being said, we all come into the Christian life with baggage from our childhood, whether it is from our actions and reactions in dealing with our parents, or the problems we faced in our adolescence, or our reactions to others who sin against us. We must remember that even if troubles and sins happen to us or affect us, we are still accountable for our lives. We cannot let those situations dictate our lives. Just like Joseph had no part in the sin that was against him, he was still responsible for his actions toward his brothers, no matter what their actions were against him. The Bible states in Proverbs 20:11, "Even a child is known by his doings, whether his work be pure, and whether it be right." We are all personally responsible for our actions. We as believers in Christ cannot let anything negative from these early years form our present Christian walk.

When we get saved, we then have a Shepherd to help in the valleys of life. God can reverse all of our baggage from childhood if we look to Him. This process is not automatic, but is developed as we trust the Lord in our valleys, and then over time, the automatic response comes as we grow in the Lord.

Our View of God

If we come from a home life where our parents never trusted in the Lord, the home was wrecked from divorce, or there was no love or acceptance, I have found that often it can affect our view of God. Our view of the Lord is the heartbeat of the Christian life. Many of us formulate a view of God when we are young in the natural man (unsaved). After we are saved, if we have not grown in the Lord and in our new relationship with Him, we can interpret God's watch care by this faulty view of God. Many times, this faulty view of God can be based out of our earthly father's care of us or another significant relationship.

Many times, God uses earthly relationships to picture our relationships with Him. God uses a bride and bridegroom relationship, husband and wife relationship, a shepherd and sheep relationship, and a father and son relationship. I believe He does this because we can relate so well to these earthly relationships and compare them to our relationship with Him.

The Lord demonstrated this in Hebrews 12:9-10:

> Furthermore we have had fathers of our flesh which corrected us, and we gave them reverence: shall we not much rather be in subjection unto the Father of spirits, and live? For they verily for a few days chastened us after their own pleasure; but he for our profit, that we might be partakers of his holiness.

Our fathers disciplined us, and God said if we listened to them, He deserves even that much more respect because He disciplines us out of love and for our good. This implies here, that Biblically, there can be a correlation between our view of the earthly father and the Heavenly Father. I believe that is why God instructs us in Ephesians 6:4, "And, ye fathers, provoke not your children to wrath: but bring them up in the nurture and admonition of the Lord." How would we provoke our children to wrath? I believe this application is carried out by us administering the wrong discipline and example.

The nurture and admonition of the Lord is descriptive of God's love and mercy in His chastisement. The result is that, if we, as earthly fathers, do not apply this kind of *loving* instruction to them, they will be provoked to wrath. We show them, while they are young, how a loving Lord disciplines them through the daddy and child relationship that we have with them. When we look at Hebrews 12, we see that God even states that, many times, fathers do not discipline correctly with the right heart, which could provoke the children to wrath. But we are also commanded to make sure that we also discipline correctly and efficiently. Just like the Bible teaches us in Proverbs 23:14, "Thou shalt beat him with the rod, and shalt deliver his soul from hell." In summary, we are to show the children a well rounded view of authority, discipline, and love because one day they will be under the authority of the Heavenly Father.

It is not uncommon for a young lady to marry someone like her father if she had a good relationship with him. In contrast, if she did not have a good relationship with her father, then often, she will do a knee jerk reaction and marry someone completely opposite. There are even a few times when a young lady will marry someone like her father, though he was not a good example. This again shows that early relationships affect future relationships.

When we come into this Shepherd/sheep relationship after we are saved, there is a danger that we will naturally respond to the Lord and His direction, similarly, to the closest earthly relationship in which we have to compare to (When I say naturally, I speak of the old nature and not the new nature.) because we have not grown in our Heavenly Father and child relationship.

Illustrating this point, let us suppose that your earthly father was a mean, abusive, unappreciative, and degrading father to you. Consequently, your relationship suffered because of him. I would almost guarantee that when you get in a valley where you are not walking with the Lord (in the new man), and you don't have the right perspective, you may naturally struggle with viewing the valleys, and you may also struggle, at times, with feeling God's dealing with you as mean, unappreciative, and degrading also. This is not an excuse to not to walk through the valleys and to blame your parents, but a mandate to trust the Lord, because, if you have been saved, you have a new nature guided by the Spirit of God. As bad as our parents may have been, we have a Great Heavenly Father, in which we cannot find fault.

We are not to continue to be a product of our past, but a product of who we are as Christians and of our relationship with our Shepherd. As difficult as it may be, there comes a point when we need to quit using our past as an excuse and walk in the victory that is afforded to us in Christ, which is our only hope. I personally don't believe that we need to dig around in our past, resurfacing old hurts, to get a better perspective in our life. I know and have experience that if we forgive the past hurts, and put them under the Blood of Christ, and walk with Him, we will be transformed.

We, as Christians, have a new life in Christ, and this puts all the situations in life in a new perspective: past, present, and future. This new life is not a re-treading of the old life, but it is a complete new start in Christ Jesus, our Saviour. The Bible states, "Therefore if any man be in Christ, he is a new creature: old things are passed away; behold, all things are become new" (2 Corinthians 5:17). This new life spoken of is applicable whether you are eight or eighty years old. This new life in Christ deals with the saving of a person's soul and, consequently, earthly destruction, because of bondage to sin.

When we are born, we are sinners (Romans 3:23), and from the time we are born physically, our bodies, minds, and personalities grow. The Lord says, "that ye put off concerning the former conversation the old man, which is corrupt according to the deceitful lusts" (Ephesians 4:22). We are commanded to put him off, and put on the new man. "And that ye put on the new man, which after God is created in righteousness and true holiness" (Ephesians 4:24).

This act of putting off and putting on is a form of repentance. Webster defines repentance as, "A change of mind, or a conversion from sin to God."[12] Likewise, it is a turning from sin to God from that which is wrong to that which is right. Acts 17:30 says, "And the times of this ignorance God winked at; but now commandeth all men every where to repent."

We live in a sinful world that feeds our sinful nature. The more we feed the old man, the more he grows and the larger the contrast and entrapment into sin our lives can become. At the moment of salvation, we become a new creature. However, the old man still resides in our lives. Galatians 5:17 explains this truth, "For the flesh lusteth against the Spirit, and the Spirit against the flesh: and these are contrary the one to the other: so that ye cannot do the things that ye would."

At the point of salvation, we have the new nature that needs to lead us by the Spirit of God. The old man is still in our life, but he is led by experience and feelings.

When we, as Christians, put our trust in the Lord and respond correctly, and see God's working, then our commitment to the Lord only gets deeper and stronger in the new man, which is led by the Spirit of God, the Word of God, and His plan.

As the new man grows up in Christ, we find that the Shepherd is loving, affirming, accepting, and always there for us. The old man loses his grip over our conduct. We begin to be in tune with the new nature rather than the old nature. In our lives, we become men and women of character rather than of circumstances of our old lives.

Character is the key to who we are in Christ. Character is who you are when no one else is around. I love this quote, "Character, not circumstances, makes the man" (Booker T. Washington).

Unfortunately, we can choose to live in the old man rather than the new man. Even if we put on the new man and love and serve the Lord for years, if the valley gets deep enough, we can revert back to the old man, at times. Then we will see that the addictions, attitudes, problems, and depressions that we had before we got saved will be evident in our lives because we are not guided by the new man.

The Bible commands us in Ephesians 4:14, "That we henceforth be no more children, tossed to and fro, and carried about with every wind of doctrine, by the sleight of men, and cunning craftiness, whereby they lie in wait to deceive;" We are to be spiritual adults, living for our Heavenly Father. "And because ye are sons, God hath sent forth the Spirit of his Son into your hearts, crying, Abba, Father" (Galatians 4:6).

As a person told me one day, "Preacher, that makes for good preaching, but hard living." He was only

> **"Character, not circumstances, makes the man." (Booker T. Washington)**

partly correct in his statement. He was right in that, if we try to walk through the valley in the power of our own flesh, life is hard.

Something to think about is the fact that if we did not have the power to save ourselves, we will not have the power and ability to sanctify ourselves, which means to set apart ourselves for the Lord. Putting off the old man and putting on the new man is the act of changing the compass and character of our actions, and now act and react from our right relationship with the Lord rather than our flesh. As Jesus said, "…the spirit indeed is willing, but the flesh is weak" (Matt 26:41). May the Lord bless you and keep you during all your valleys, as you walk in the new man.

How to Come into the Fold and Get Identity with the Shepherd

When it comes to keeping everything in perspective, there is a critical point that needs to be addressed. Maybe you have read this and you don't have the Shepherd in your heart to lead and direct you. I purposely put this subject at the end because I wanted to show you throughout the book what the Christian life is all about, being in a Shepherd and Sheep relationship. You may have already assumed that you do not have this type of relationship with God. You may believe that there is a God, but just believing that there is a God is not enough. The Bible states that you must be born again. "Jesus answered and said unto him, Verily, verily, I say unto thee, Except a man be born again, he cannot see the kingdom of God" (John 3:3).

This is the new nature that I was just talking about earlier. Being born again means that I have a new life in Christ. The born again experience happens when God deals with your heart about your condition of sinfulness. "For all have sinned, and come short of the glory of God" (Romans 3:23). This means that all have sinned against God and are guilty of sin.

The Bible states we are born sinners, as stated in Romans 5:12, "Wherefore, as by one man [ADAM] sin entered into the world, and death by sin; and so death passed upon all men, for that all have sinned:" From the time we are born, we sin. Our parents never taught us to sin; it came about naturally. Sin is any action, reaction, or deed against what God has decreed wrong. This includes all of God's commandments in the Bible.

Once God deals with us regarding our sin, this will also reveal our need to do something about our sin. Romans 6:23 says, "For the wages of sin is death; but the gift of God is eternal life through Jesus Christ our Lord." Since we are sinners, there is a judgment for sin, and this judgment is death. Our sin brings about death.

Back in the book of Genesis, in Genesis 2:17, God tells Adam and Eve, "But of the tree of the knowledge of good and evil, thou shalt not eat of it: for in the day that thou eatest thereof thou shalt surely die." From that moment on, for all humanity, there would be a physical death because of sin, as well as a spiritual death in a place that Jesus called Hell.

As we have looked so far, we are sinners and are doomed to death. However, the Bible states in Romans 6:23, "...but the gift of God is eternal life through Jesus Christ our Lord." This free gift that God has given us is salvation from our sinful condition. Now, like any gift, we must personally receive it in order for it to become ours.

We must receive Christ as stated in John 1:12, "But as many as received him, to them gave he power to become the sons of God, even to them that believe on his name:"

We must know our condition and believe in Christ. That is, believing what Romans 10:9 says, "That if thou shalt confess with thy mouth the Lord Jesus, and shalt believe in thine heart that God hath raised him from the dead, thou shalt be saved." We believe that Christ came to save us by taking our penalty of our sin on Himself. He paid the penalty with the cross by dying our death for us. So we must believe in our hearts that this is true, and that Jesus, God Himself, came and died for us. Also, we must believe that Jesus rose from the dead. In 1 Corinthians 15:14, it says, "And if Christ be not risen, then is our preaching vain, and your faith is also vain." Our faith is in God's provisions for our sin and His power over death.

The Bible goes on to say in Romans 10:10, "...For with the heart man believeth unto righteousness; and with the mouth confession is made unto salvation." You must believe in your heart that Jesus came, died, rose again three days later and lives at the right Hand of the Father, and you must be willing to put your faith in what Jesus did for you. This faith is in our hearts. Similarly, just like we have faith that our physical heart is working fine right now, we also have assurance that it will beat again when we need it to. Your life depends on it. Likewise, you know that Jesus is your only Hope, and that you are putting your life, death, and eternity in what He did. You know that you cannot do it yourself with your works, as stated in Ephesians 2:8, "For by grace are ye saved through faith; and that not of yourselves: it is the gift of God." You cannot save yourself. You must have the Lord. The smallest sin will keep us from Heaven, outside of a relationship with Christ before salvation. I had a person say to me once, "I am not a sinner because I have only committed little sins in my life." I responded to them by asking, "Would you consider eating of a piece of fruit in a garden without permission, a little sin?" They responded, "Yes, that would be a small sin!" I answered, "Well, this small sin, as you call it, plunged man into sin and death; and this little sin was the reason that Jesus Christ had to come and die on the cross. So, there really are no small sins to God."

So once I:
- Realize my sin
- Recognize my responsibility
- Realize Jesus' gift

Then I need to:
- Receive that gift of salvation provided through the death, burial, and resurrection.

As you know, salvation is of your heart. You need to seal the deal by calling out to God in prayer and telling the Lord something like this:

"Lord Jesus, I know that I am a sinner and guilty before God. I know that You came to earth to die for me as the means of forgiveness of sin. I believe that You rose again the third day and are alive in Heaven today. I repent of my sins, and I receive the free gift of salvation by placing my faith in the finished work of the Cross. I give my heart to You this day _____. Thank You for coming into my heart and saving me."

Once you pray from your heart and confess, you enter into this relationship with the Almighty God. You have a new life in Christ. Much of what we have already discussed can now become a reality in your life. You need to go back to the section about, *Being What You Are Supposed to Be,* and read what a normal Christian does, like getting into a Gospel preaching church, reading your Bible, and praying to your Shepherd and Saviour. Now, you can finally have a Shepherd to lead, guide, and direct you.

Conclusion

Through this book, we have seen that we can make it through the valleys. These valleys are a part of our Christian life. God will use these valleys if we allow Him. He is our Shepherd and we are His sheep. He will provide for us according to His will and what is best for us. The Shepherd leads us through the valleys of life with a divine purpose and outcome, painting a picture in our lives with a road map guided through the Word of God and with godly people to support us along our way. Let the valleys and trials take a new purpose in our lives, and let us not see them any more as stumbling blocks, but instead, let's accept these valleys as stepping stones to a greater faith and trust in our Shepherd.

I told you the story of the preacher earlier, and promised to finish it. Remember that his daughter died when she was only three years old, and his marriage was destroyed? He started drinking and lost everything. He had an education in theology, but then he turned to alcohol in the valley rather than to the Lord. He took his eyes off God, and thus he fell into alcoholism. However, he got back up, and God has greatly used him since. The way that God worked in this man's life and turned him around, was that He directed this man's eyes on the Lord Jesus Christ, so he could find peace and joy in the Shepherd rather than the bottle. He now works in a home for people with substance abuses and is a great blessing to many.

I finish this story for a purpose. Like this man that I described, maybe you have fallen by the wayside during the valley. Just get back on the narrow road and trust in the Lord. As we appeal to the Great Shepherd for all our problems, let us run to Him, and

He will take care of us.

In closing, I leave you with a great illustration of our loving Shepherd and His eagerness to bind up our wounds from the valleys of our lives. The following story out of E.M. Bounds' book *Prayer and Faith*, speaks of a friend of Bounds, who was a hunter, who got connected with his softer side when confronted by a fawn one day.

Rising early one morning, he said, I heard the baying of a score of deerhounds in pursuit of their quarry. Looking away to a broad, open field in front of me, I saw a young fawn making its way across, and giving signs, moreover, that its race was well-nigh run. Reaching the rails of the enclosure, it leaped over and crouched within ten feet from where I stood. A moment, later two of the hounds came over, when the fawn ran in my direction and pushed its head between my legs. I lifted the little thing to my breast, and, swinging round and round, fought off the dogs. I felt, just then, that all the dogs in the West could not, and should not capture that fawn after its weakness had appealed to my strength.' So is it, when human helplessness appeals to Almighty God. Well do I remember when the hounds of sin were after my soul, until, at last, I ran into the arms of Almighty God.[13]

ENDNOTES

1. Ralph Gower, _The New manners & Customs of Bible times._ Singapore. 1933.143

2. Elmer Towns, _Praying the 23rd Psalm._ Minneapolis: Regal, 2001. 79.

3. Albert Barnes, _originally published Notes on the Old Testament, Explanatory and Practical,_ 1832-1872. Psalm 23:4.

4. Greg Olsen, _The Lord is My Shepherd._ Milwaukee WI: Ideals Publishing,1957.49

5. Charles Spurgeon, _Morning by Morning_ 1866. 04/29/AM

6. A.W. Tozer, _We Travel an Appointed Way_ (Camp Hill, PA: Christian Publications, 1988),3-4.

7. _Today in the Word,_ May, 1990, MBI, p. 34

8. John Gill, _John Gill's Exposition of the Entire Bible,_ 1690-1771. Genesis 50:20

9. T.C. Pinkney, _Remarks to the Southern Baptist Convention Executive Committee,_ Nashville, Tennessee, September 18, 2001.

10. Vance Havner, _Fourscore_ (Old Tappan, NJ: Revell, 1982), 23.

11. Rhonda Harrington Kelly, _Divine Discipline How to Develop and Maintain Self Control,_ Gretna: Pelican Publishing, 1992. 147.

12. Noah Webster, _American Dictionary of the English Language,_ 1828

13. E.M. Bounds, _Books on Prayer by E. M. Bounds_ (1835-1913)

SUPPLEMENTAL RESOURCES
Personal Study
Small Groups
Sunday School, Etc.

Based on Chapters 1-7

These lessons are available for download at:
www.jerrybeaver.net/walkingthroughthevalleysoflife.html

For personal study, a notebook will be helpful.

Check out: www.jerrybeaver.net

STUDY 1
THE VALLEY OF PURPOSE
The Shepherd and Sheep Relationship
Based on Chapter One
PSALM 23

As we embark on the study, *Walking Through the Valleys of Life,* let us keep in mind that all the answers to life are found in the Word of God. Our Heavenly Father has a relationship with us and loves us greatly enough to send His Son to die on the cross for our sins and salvation. Thus, He has given us a new life in Him. May we claim His promises and love, walking in the newness and victory of the Lord.

Our study will be based out of Psalm 23, with emphasis put on Jesus being the Great Shepherd and we, as Christians, being His sheep. Many in the world try to claim the promises of this great text without knowing and following the Shepherd. However, you cannot claim promises that don't apply to you. As a child of God you *can* claim them. So, let's follow the Shepherd and rest in His provisions, looking to Him and not the valley's darkness and depth.

I. THE SHEPHERD AND SHEEP RELATIONSHIP
READ PSALM 23

Verse 1

Here we see the opening illustration of the Shepherd and Sheep Relationship. The shepherd's purpose was to be the caregiver and protector of the flock. "Shall not want" implies that God can and will provide for His Sheep.

Verse 2

This text speaks to the kind of provisions that come from the shepherd. "Green pastures" speak of the bountiful blessings that come from God. "Still waters" refer to the provisions needed by the finicky and timid sheep that, many times, would not drink from a rushing stream.

Verse 3

In this portion of the Psalm, we see the restoration by the Lord, the taking, taming, teaching, and securing of wild sheep, and we see the new purpose of the sheep's lives.

Verse 4

Here we find the lives of the sheep under the protection of the Shepherd. The valley of the shadow of death speaks to the dark valleys of our lives in which we become fearful and often make bad decisions. In this verse, we find a promise that we don't have to be fearful, but we can be guided by the Hand of God.

Verse 5

We find here that God will lead us into situations and circumstances that would make the average person feel uncomfortable. (Namely, being surrounded by our enemies.) But God will take uncomfortable situations and make them into great blessings if we stay with the Shepherd.

Verse 6

Here we find the summation of the life that we have as sheep of the Great Shepherd. "Surely goodness and mercy shall follow me." Meaning, that God is going to be with me through all the circumstances of life, as I follow and serve Him.

II. THE VALLEY
PSALM 23:4

---

1. I will walk through valleys in my life, and many of those valleys are a part of God's working (Job 5:7, John 11 Lazarus' death, Psalms 119:67-68, 71-72).
    *   How has the Lord used the valleys in your life?
    *   What good has come from them?

2. The valleys become more painful when we doubt God's love for us or question His intention for the valleys that are in our lives (Philippians 2:13, John 3:16, 1 Peter 1:6-7).
    *   When have you doubted God's provisions for your needs?
    *   Write out how you have doubted His love.

3. We must allow ourselves to be led by the Shepherd and not fall to the temptation of trying to lead Him (Rom 12:1- 2, Amos 3:3).
    *   Consider some situations where it might be tempting to try to lead God.

4. Everyone has valleys, no matter if they are Christians or not (Matthew 5:45).
    *   How have you compared your life with others'?
    *   Why is this wrong?

5. Your reactions in the valley speak volumes of your relationship with the Shepherd (Matthew 7:16-17).
    *   What are your reactions saying about you currently?
    *   What have your past valleys said about your relationship with the Lord?

6. The fact that God is with us all the time as our Shepherd should

move us to an introspective life (Psalm 139:7-11).
- What does it mean to you, personally, to have God always with you?

7. God's chastening in the valley (rod) is comforting and assuring (Hebrews 12:6, James 1:2-4).
   - List some reasons why chastening would be comforting.

8. God did not intend for the valleys of life to dictate our decisions, but His perfect will should solely guide us (Provebs 3:5-6, Psalms 27:13-14).
   - Can you find some Scriptures that teach God's Guidance?

9. God knows how to provide for all our needs at all times (Matt 6:25-34, Philippians 4:6-7).
   - Think back to your last major valley (or use one that you are in currently). How did God provide for your physical, emotional, and spiritual needs?

10. God's provisions are based on His will for us. Our Christian lives are not made to order, and righteousness is always a primary purpose in our lives.
    - When has God provided for You in His own way?
    - How long did it take for you to recognize the benefits?

III. THE PURPOSE
READ PSALM 23:5-8, ROMANS 8:28

---

1. We need to remember that the valleys of life have a purpose and divine approval. (Proverbs 16:4-31,19:21, 20:24).
   - What are some of the purposes that you have realized in your valleys?
   - How have you recognized that your valley had divine approval?

2. Valleys produced faith in the Lord, and faith is the only way to serve the Lord (Hebrews 10:23, 11:6, Psalms 37:1-7).
   - List some areas that the Lord has built your faith in Him during the valleys of life.

3. At times, the Lord may allow hurt in your life, but He will not harm you (Psalms 119:67, 71).
   - How have your stressful situations in life hurt?
   - How has the Lord eased the pain of those hurts?

4. God allows some things that have to be worked out only through Him, so that we may experience His presence (Matthew 17:19-21).
   - How has God shown His presence through your valleys?

5. A faith that is not tested cannot be trusted (Hebrews 11).
   - How has my faith been tested, and what has the test revealed.

Walking Through the Valleys of Life

Study 2
THE VALLEY IS GOD'S HALLWAY
Based on Chapter Two

The second study of *Walking Through the Valleys of Life*, deals with our perspective of the valleys. In other words, how one views and deals with the particular valleys that God has allowed. Most of the truths that we learned from Study One are truths that we know, but we have a hard time putting them to practice. In this lesson, as well as future lessons, we will look at how to practically and scripturally make our valleys victorious.

As you look at this lesson about making God's valleys a hallway, consider that a valley is a path between the mountains. Though valleys can be negative, literally, many times, mountains would be impassable if it were not for the valleys' paths. The same is true with life. Valleys are a part of God's economy in our lives. We need to look at them as hallways to God's blessings in which paths may be rough, but the ending will be great with the Lord in control.

Psalms 23:4 Yea, though I walk through the <u>valley</u> of the <u>shadow of death,</u> I will fear no evil: for thou art with me; thy rod and thy staff they comfort me.

I. TURNING A VALLEY INTO A HALLWAY

---

1. Valleys are literally made because of the water running to the bottom of the mountains and flowing to the least path of resistance. This water carves out the trail through the mountain which gets deeper over time. When we observe our lives and valleys, the valleys are running their course and molding us as Christians, likewise, shaping our lives after Christ. This molding and shaping is a process that takes time. Therefore, we don't need to be fearful of the valleys because the valleys are just God's working in my life (2 Timothy 1:7, Mark 4:39-40).
    *   List the ways that you have expected your life to be easy?
    *   What should have been your thinking?

2. The shadow of death is just that, "a shadow." We need not to be fearful, but we must remain faithful unto the Lord (Luke 12:5-7, Romans 8:15, 2 Timothy 1:7).
    *   Has the valley that you're in, or future valley made you fearful of death?
    *   Why do you think this fear is in your life?

1. Many times, we get impatient and want to be relieved or

II. DON'T RUN IN GOD'S HALLWAY
Isaiah 40:31

---

delivered from the valley, which was David's cry in his distress (Psalms 55:6).
    *   How has your response been similar to David's?
    *   What can be learned from your wrong attitude?

2. The Lord is not in a hurry. We, however, usually are in a big rush to get through difficult times. Our fear drives us to run, thinking we can run from our valley. We may, at times, fear, but our fear should drive us to have faith in the Lord. This is part of the

purpose for the valley in the first place (Isaiah 43:2).
- How has your fear driven you through the valley?
- Can you find a verse in the Bible that deals with no fearing? *Hint 2 Timothy 1:?*

3. We need to understand that we are in the valley for the duration, and our running out of the valleys will get us no where (Psalm 27:14).
- Have you wanted to run from the valley in your life? How so?
- Was there a certain element of the valley that made you want to run? What is the biblical response to your fear?

4. To run out of the valley would be to miss the grandeur of God's provision and watch care. Psalm 23:4 says that we will "walk through the valley of the shadow of death." This is indicative that we are walking together (Amos 3:3).
- How have you and the Lord walked together through your valley?
- List specific ways where you have felt God's presence in past or present valleys.

III. NO PARKING AND POUTING
HEBREWS 13:5

---

1. Many Christians use the valley as an excuse to justify complacency. An example of this is Jonah, when he became depressed over God's working in the Ninevite's lives. He pouted under the juniper tree. This was just as bad as him running from his valley when God called him to go at the beginning of the story which landed him in the belly of the whale.
- What prompted Jonah to park and pout?
- In what ways have you done the same thing in your valley?

2. Any wrong reaction to God's directed plan in the valley is very

ineffective and destructive (Judges 21:25).
- Make a list of some of your unbiblical reactions.

3. To become complacent in the valley can make us a sitting duck to the Devil (1 Peter 5:8).
   - In what ways has Satan attacked you in the valley?

4. Being complacent in the valley breeds stagnation in our lives; thus our complacency causes us to lose our effectiveness because God's trying to use the valley to shine His light through us (Matt 5:13).
   - What is your definition of being complacent in the valley?

5. We must be careful not to use the excuse that we are waiting on the Lord to justify our lack of moving forward for the Lord (Hebrews 12:1).
   - What are some of the excuses that you have made in the most troublesome times of your life?

6. The way that we keep from parking, pouting, and running in the valley is to confirm that we are walking with the Lord through the hallway that He has allowed, and knowing that it has a divine approval. If God has allowed the valley/hallway in our lives, then He can sustain us through it. I think about Daniel and the lion's den (Daniel 6). Daniel marched in by faith; he did not fight them, nor did he run, but he trusted that if the Lord had allowed this valley, then the Lord would carry him through it. See also the three Hebrew children (Daniel 3).
   - How does this truth apply to your situation?

Walking Through the Valleys of Life

Study 3
THE LIGHT AT THE END OF TUNNEL
Based on Chapter Three

This study starts with the premise that everything that happens in our lives is allowed by God. This truth concludes that God has a planned outcome. Accepting this truth changes our perspectives and gives us hope in the darkest of valleys.

In every situation, there is hope, as long as the Lord is with us. There will be times when we get nervous, but this emotion can drive us to look at why our Shepherd has allowed this valley in our lives. Hope is something that doesn't develop out of thin air but needs to be substantiated in something. For us, a sheep of the Great Shepherd, our hope is rooted in the loving, guided, and sovereign relationship with the Master.

I. THE DARKNESS
Ephesians 5:8

---

1. We don't need to be fearful of the darkness as long as we remember that if the shadows are so dark that you cannot see, we <u>know</u> the Lord is still with us.
   - What valleys, past or present, have been so dark that you could not see any light? List them.
   - How would you counsel someone to help them see that the Lord was still with them?

2. If I cannot see Him, I know that He can see me and has my life covered (Psalms 121:4, 1 Thessalonians 5:4, 9, Hebrews 13:5).
   - List a few examples of the dark times in your life, present or past.

3. Jesus is the Door Keeper of our lives. Just like when the sheep would bed down at night in the caves, the shepherd (Jesus) would sleep prostrate in the opening of the cave (John 10:7).
   - Do you realize that the Great Shepherd is always with you?
   - In what ways would you suppose God has protected you in the valley?

4. In the darkness of life there is always a light, and that light is God's divine outcome. Though the light may be small, we need to pray for God to reveal it and help us walk toward it (Psalms 23:3, Romans 12:1-2).
   - Write out or pray out loud a prayer asking the Lord to reveal the light to you and to give you the strength to go toward the light.

5. The darkness in the valley is a test to show us if we are truly trusting in the Lord. Like taking a test in school, my grade reveals how much of the information I have retained. So, also, my faith during the valley reveals how much trust I have in the Lord (1 Peter 1:7, James 1:4).

- What has my valley, past or present, revealed to me about my faith?
- What is my reaction to my spiritual grade?

6. If we love God and are called according to His purpose, the Bible states that all things work together for good. Like working a puzzle, we work it one piece at a time with the big picture in mind (Romans 8:28, Philippians 1:12).
   - Looking at my valleys, what have I learned about the big picture in hindsight?

II. THE HOPE AND FOCUS OF THE LIGHT
1 Peter 1:3

---

1. If God led you into the valley, then He will lead you out (Philippians 2:13).
   - In what ways has God led you into the valley?
   - How would you project that God may lead you out of the valley?

2. There is a focus of the valley, meaning that there is a primary purpose for the valley in my life. The focus is a trial or test, a temptation, and/or chastisement from the Lord (1 Peter 1:7, Hebrews 12:6-8, James 1:12).
   - Which of your valleys were for the purpose of a test, temptation, or chastisement from the Lord?
   - Did you respond correctly? What could you have done differently?

3. When we go back to those times that we have quit in the valleys or wanted to, what actually happens is, we give up on God. Sometimes we don't even recognize that we are quitting because we, seemingly, cannot figure out what He is doing presently. Such was the case with David (Psalm 22).

   - What are some of the things about your valleys that

make you want to quit?

- Can you recognize when you are ready to quit? If yes, what are the signs?

4. 1 Corinthians 10:13 is often misconstrued and taken out of context. This verse means that God will not put more on you than you can bear when you are trusting in Him. However, if you are not trusting God, then you are bearing the weight yourself. If you're walking in the flesh, you will not be equipped to carry the load of the valley.

- How have I relied on my own strength in the valleys?

STUDY 4
GOD'S PAINTING THE BIG PICTURE IN THE VALLEY
Based on Chapter Four

Study number four deals with how God is working in and through our valley to bring about something beautiful in our lives. This beauty is found in the righteousness that the valley will produce (Psalm 23:2) and the glory that is brought to the Lord, as well as the help that it produces to others through the valley.

Many times, as God moves in our lives, the picture may seem unclear at first. Just like a painter painting a picture, each stroke of the brush adds another part of the big picture. The adventure of the valley is that each part reveals God's overall working in my life. As we study this lesson, may God reveal what He has done in our lives through past valleys, as well as revealing to us what He possibly will be doing in the future.

I. WHO IS THE PAINTING FOR?

---

1. Artists have a purpose behind each painting that they create. Our purpose, as sheep of the Great Shepherd, is to be a light for Him in this world. Likewise, our lives take twists and turns in order for God to work in us, to use our lives in others, and to fulfill God's purposes on this earth through us (John 11 Lazarus, Job).

    - Has your valley started producing anything in your life? Why or why not?
    - Who else has been helped by your valley?

2. The light that breaks through in the valley develops the picture. The more light that is given, the more the picture becomes visible. The Word of God is the source of light (Proverbs 4:18, 2 Peter 2:10, Psalms 119:105).

    - What are some ways that you have seen the Lord's light shining in your valleys?
    - List a few ways that your valley might paint a picture in your life in the end?

3. Joseph is a good example of several twists and turns in a long deep valley. As each step in the darkness was taken, it brought a beautiful picture of God's forgiveness and restoration (Genesis 50:20).

    - How does your life resemble the life of Joseph?
    - Outline the various steps of your valleys past or present.

    Example from Joseph's life:

    1. Thrown in a pit

    2. Sold into slavery

    3. Seduction from Potiphar's wife

    4. Prison

    5. Deliverance

    6. Leadership

    7. Saving the Brethren

Walking Through the Valleys of Life

STUDY 5
THE CRUTCHES IN THE VALLEYS
Based on Chapter Five

It is so easy to stop trusting the Lord during the valleys of our lives. We use "crutches" to lean on during our valleys. Meaning, we trust in other things during a valley rather than the Lord. These would be sins, people, or an attitude. The problems with these crutches are that they give us a false solace and trust. We miss the big purpose of the valley, which is trusting in the Lord.

As the Bible states:

> Matthew 11:28-30, "Come unto me, all ye that labour and are heavy laden, and I will give you rest. Take my yoke upon you, and learn of me; for I am meek and lowly in heart: and ye shall find rest unto your souls. For my yoke is easy, and my burden is light."

I. THE CRUTCH OF SIN

---

1. Sin is literally rebellion against God, and because we don't trust in God in the valleys of life, there is much pain associated with many of our valleys. The fact that there is pleasure in sin for a short time makes it very appetizing (Hebrews 11:25). Though we get instant relief from sin, the relief, however, is not lasting (Numbers 32:23).

   • What kind of crutches have you leaned on in your past and present valleys?
   • What relief did you expect them to give?
   • What truth will keep you from seeking out these crutches in the future?

2. Sin separates us from God and the voice of the Shepherd, which, consequently, is dangerous for the sheep in the valley (Psalm 66:16).

   • Has sin separated you from the Shepherd in the valley? How so?

II. THE CRUTCH OF DEATH

---

1. Death is often looked at as a way of escape rather than trusting and fixing our mentality toward the valley (Psalms 55:6). Paul thought he was going to die, but he lived many years afterwards (2 Timothy 4:6). Job wished he had never been born (Job 3:1-3).

   • Has your valley been so bad that you wanted to just give up on life?
   • From what you have already learned, what should be your thinking about this matter?

2. God gives life, and God takes life away. Our lives are not up to us (Job 1:21).

   • What reminds you that your life is not your own?

III. THE CRUTCH OF DENIAL

1. Denial in the valley is when we are not willing to admit that we are in a bad place at all. This mentality is not an honest thought and also a neglect of the working of God in our lives.

    - In what ways have you denied that you're in a valley?
    - What is your present valley? Try writing a letter to the Lord. Tell Him the details of your hurts, your wants, and your needs. This will enable you to process all the details of the valley, and at the same time, eliminate any chance of denial of your problems.

2. In Jeremiah 6:9-15, the people did not want to admit that they were in trouble with the Lord and under His chastisement.

    - Has the Lord been chastising you over a response in the valley? If yes, how so?

IV. THE CRUTCH OF EXPERIENCE

Often, in the Scriptures, we are commanded to have wisdom, but wisdom is not to replace full dependence on the Lord. We do not walk through future valleys in life in the same manner as we have walked in past valleys (Proverbs 3:5, Philippians 3:18).

- In what ways have you depended on your experience rather than God's direction?
- What has been the result?

STUDY 6
THE MAP IN THE VALLEY
Based on Chapter Six

Wouldn't it be nice if all the details of our valley would be laid out for us? I really don't think so, for if we knew where some valleys were going to lead us, we might never persevere through them. God only gives us the details and instructions in the valleys on a need to know basis. Each step of faith prepares us to take the next step of faith in God's will.

Our final destination is Heaven, but the time frame from when we get saved and get to Heaven could be many years. So, we plod along, not wanting and expecting the details upfront, but we listen for the Lord's voice and guidance. In this study, we will focus on God directing and guiding us through the valleys which He has allowed.

I. TURN BY TURN DIRECTIONS

1. A complete map may not be what is best for us. It may become obsolete in the middle of the journey as God reroutes our lives and the purpose in the valley (Job 13:15).
   - Has the Lord rerouted your valley?
   - What would you suppose the purpose would have changed to in the valley? If so, how?
2. God's providence demands that the map in the valley needs to be alterable, not that it is always changeable, but God, in His Sovereignty, has given man a choice, and our choices can affect God and even His will for our lives (1Thessalonians 2:18, 2 Timothy 4:14, Matthew 13:58).
   - How has your decisions affected the Lord's purpose in the valley?

II. WATCH OUT COMPLAINING ABOUT DIRECTIONS
Numbers 11:1, Psalms 77:3

1. No stiffer judgment came upon the people of God until they complained. If you were to search out every time the people of God complained to Him and the judgment that was associated with the complaining, your findings would help you not to complain any longer (Hebrews 13:5).
   - Make a list of all the different complaints that you conjured up in the valley?
   - Try to find Scriptures that contradict the complaint.

2. Being a complainer will only worsen the directions in the valley. Our complaining puts the blame on the Lord. This breaks the heart of the Lord when He has supplied all the direction that we need (Luke 12:6-7, Genesis 6:6).
   - Write out an apology letter to the Lord about the complaining that you have done.

III. THE WORD AND THE SPIRIT: READING THE MAP
2 Timothy 3:16

---

1. Reading the map in the valley is, basically, taking what we know (the Word of God) and the direction from the Lord, which comes through the Spirit of God, and then putting it to action in our lives (2 Peter 2:19).
   - Write out a paragraph or so about how the Bible speaks to your past or present valleys. Then tell how you plan to put what you know into action.

2. The Spirit of God is the interpreter of the Word and helps us apply the Word to our lives (John15:26, 16:13, Matthew 4:1).
   - When has the Word of God been illuminated for you by the Holy Spirit? What were the Scriptures, and how did they speak to you?

3. The Word and Spirit will always lead you to live by faith (Hebrews 11:6).
   - How has your faith increased through your valley?

IV. THE SCOPE AND LIMITED MAP IN THE VALLEY

---

1. There is a direct purpose for the valley, but there can be multiple benefactors from our valleys (Genesis 50:20).
   - Make a list of the people that could be possible benefactors of your valleys.

2. God may be using a valley in your life in many other people's lives. Such was the case with Nehemiah and his valley.
   - From the prior list, expound in detail how you would think that God would use your valley in their lives.

V. OUR INDIVIDUAL MAP

---

1. God has a call and a direct purpose for your individual life (Jeremiah 1:5, Psalms 139:14).
   - What do you think is the direct purpose for your life and for your past or present valley?

2. We cannot compare how God has led or is leading us with another servant of God. God has a special plan for each one of His sheep (Luke 12:32, Ephesians 1:5, 2 Corinthians 10:12).
   - When have you been guilty of comparing your hurts and valleys with other people? Why is that wrong?

VI. ANGELS' HELP
Hebrews 13:2, Genesis 19:1

Just as God has directed all His servants, God can and wants to direct you. He will even send some help in the form of His angels to help you along the way.

- Are there any ways that you can see that God as led angels to help you along the way?

STUDY 7
PREPARATION FOR THE JOURNEY
Based on Chapter Seven

As we finish this study, we want to discuss how we can prepare for life's valleys. Much has already been covered, but, in this study, we will talk about key points that help prepare for the many valleys in life. There are many valleys in life, but the answer is the same. The answer is a firm and confident walk with the Lord, marching into the valleys that are dark and deep with assurance that God is with us.

2 Timothy 3:16 "All scripture is given by inspiration of God, and is profitable for doctrine, for reproof, for correction, for instruction in righteousness:"

I. VARIOUS VALLEYS
Job 5:7

Different valleys affect different parts of our lives (1 Thessalonians 5:23). The Valleys of the Mind, The Valleys of the Heart, The Valleys of the Flesh

- List your past and present valleys, and which category do they fit in?

II. BEING WHAT WE ARE SUPPOSED TO BE

1. Small valleys prepare us for larger valleys in the future (Philippians 1:6).
   - When have you seen this pattern in your own life?
2. Being a basic Christian and practicing the basic principles such as, praying, reading your Bible, being faithful to church, and walking in the Spirit will be a great resource for walking through the valleys of life. (Hebrews 10:25, 1 Peter 2:2, Romans 8:1).
   - Have any of these principles been neglected in your valleys?
   - What is your plan to reincorporate them in your walk?

3. Memorize Scriptures to help with future problems.
   - (Psalms 119:11)

4. Get in a good Bible-believing church (Hebrews 10:25, Ecclesiastes 4:12).
   - Do you have a Bible-believing church?
   - When is the last time you attended?

5. Seek godly counsel (Proverbs 15:22, Proverbs 24:6).
   - Have you sought godly counsel? How did this help?

III. DOING WHAT WE WERE DOING BEFORE THE VALLEY CAME

We should continue the things that we were doing before the valley as long as they were the right things. The best way to prepare is to just put our life in auto pilot for the Lord and not to panic (2 Timothy 3:14).

- What was your spiritual condition before your valleys, past or present?
- How did this answer affect your valley?

IV. WATCH OUT FOR SATAN
1 Peter 5:8

When preparing for the journeys through the valley, we need to be very careful to watch for Satan, knowing that God allows Satan to tempt us and even test our faith at times. Satan is always looking to take us off guard. One of the ways that we can prepare is to remember how Satan has worked in our lives by tripping us up in the past, and then we can avoid his future snares (2 Corinthians 2:11).

- How has Satan worked in the past in your valleys?
- How can you be on guard against him in the future?